Introduction to the

Guan Yin Citta Dharma Door

Title: Introduction to the Guan Yin Citta Dharma Door

Author: Master Jun Hong Lu
Proofread: Australian Chinese Buddhist Research Centre Publishing
Design: Australian Chinese Buddhist Research Centre Publishing
Production editor: Australian Chinese Buddhist Research Centre Publishing
Published by Australian Chinese Buddhist Research Centre Publishing
Address: Level 2, 54 Meagher St., Chippendale
                   Sydney NSW 2008 Australia
Phone: +61 2 9283 2758
Website: www.GuanYinCitta.com
First edition, First printing, April 2019
Serial number: 978-0-9872230-7-4
Print run: 10 000

Preface

All sutras and mantras in this book are based on the *Buddhist Recitation Collection*, compiled by Zhao Puchu, the former President of the Chinese Buddhist Association.

1. The contents of this book are constantly being updated. Please refer to our website, www.GuanYinCitta.com, for the latest information.
2. In case of any discrepancies, the latest Chinese version published on the blog, lujunhong2or.com, is to be taken as correct.
3. This book is for free distribution only, strictly not for sale.

Contents

Contents

Preface

Guan Shi Yin Bodhisattva (Guan Yin Bodhisattva, otherwise known as Guan Zi Zai Bodhisattva in Chinese, Avalokitesvara in Sanskrit) is a Bodhisattva with immense amounts of loving kindness and compassion. With immeasurable wisdom and miraculous powers, she comes to the aid of those experiencing hardship and difficulty. She attained Buddhahood countless eons ago and is known as "the Buddha of True Dharma Light". However, due to her great vow and strong affinity with sentient beings, Guan Yin Bodhisattva returned to the world to rescue all sentient beings from suffering.

Together, Guan Yin Bodhisattva, Manjusri Bodhisattva (who embodies great wisdom), Samantabhadra Bodhisattva (great practice), and Ksitigarbha Bodhisattva (great vows) are widely known as the Four Great Bodhisattvas. Guan Yin Bodhisattva is also one of the "Three Saints of the Western Pure Land," along with Amitabha Buddha and Mahasthamaprapta Bodhisattva.

Out of deep compassion, Guan Yin Bodhisattva hears the desperate cries of sentient beings and acts to relieve their suffering. She responds to all prayers, and never abandons a single life. There have been innumerable miraculous stories about Guan Yin Bodhisattva, beginning in ancient times. Hence the old Chinese saying: "Every family pays respects to Amitabha Buddha; every household prays to Guan Yin Bodhisattva."

For thousands of years, Guan Yin Bodhisattva has manifested in many different forms in order to help people. According to the *Lotus Sutra*, "If there were living beings who would be liberated by a certain form of being, then Guan Yin Bodhisattva would appear as that form of being to speak the Dharma." In Chinese history, figures said to be the manifestations of Guan Yin Bodhisattva include Liu Sa He (4th-5th century) of the Eastern Jin Dynasty, Chan Master Bao Zhi Gong (5th-6th century) of the Southern Dynasties, Venerable Master Sengqie (7th-8th century) of the Tang Dynasty and so forth. They did not shy away from using their spiritual power to perform miracles.

Today, Master Jun Hong Lu, the founder of Guan Yin Citta Dharma Door, is also widely regarded as a manifestation of Guan Yin Bodhisattva. With his Dharma eye and great spiritual power, Master Lu crystallizes the law of cause and effect and the working of karma. By performing "Totem Readings" based upon someone's year of birth, gender, and Chinese zodiac sign, he reveals their past, present and future, and points out what truly causes the ups and downs in their daily lives.

The result is immediate and obvious: For the benefit of ourselves and others, we need to refrain from doing evil and practise only good deeds. We must be mindful of our intentions and actions at every moment, and stop creating negative karma in our everyday lives. By practising Buddhism, cultivating our minds and changing our behaviour, having paid off our karmic debts and refrained from accruing new ones, we truly transform our destiny and are liberated from suffering.

Guan Yin Citta Dharma Door teaches us to repay our karmic debts by following the "Three Golden Buddhist Practices": reciting Buddhist scriptures, making great vows and performing life liberations. These practices lay a solid foundation for improved physical and mental well-being. They have also been proved to be helpful in curing illnesses, resolving interpersonal conflicts and increasing one's spiritual strength and wisdom. Due to Guan Yin Citta Dharma Door's effectiveness and efficiency, it has been taken up by 10 million people in a very short period of time.

Guan Yin Citta Dharma Door belongs to the Mahayana Buddhist tradition. It is transmitted directly by Guan Yin Bodhisattva through Master Lu. For decades, he has been devoted to spreading the message of compassion and Buddhist teachings via his radio program and the Internet.

His advice is based entirely on the teachings and practices of traditional Buddhism. Day in and day out, he has been tirelessly helping people without asking for anything in return—a powerful expression of Guan Yin Bodhisattva's compassion towards people no matter who they are or where they are from.

Introduction to Guan Yin Citta Dharma Door provides answers to common Buddhist questions, and guides those people who have an affinity with Buddhism in their practice of traditional Buddhism. As we progress in our spiritual practice, we strengthen our faith in the ability to change destiny and free ourselves from suffering. As we grow in wisdom and accumulate merits and virtues, we can transcend the prisons of ignorance, anger, fear and desire, and arrive at true inner peace and liberation.

We hope that more people can learn and practise the wonderful Buddhist practice of Guan Yin Citta Dharma Door: To embark upon Guan Yin Bodhisattva's vessel of compassion to purify minds, be free from afflictions and suffering, pay off karmic debts, help others awaken and elevate spiritually, spread the Dharma far and wide, and finally arrive at the Western Pure Land of Ultimate Bliss and the Four Sagely Realms (i.e. Sravaka, Pratyekabuddha, Bodhisattvas and Buddhas).

Secretariat
Guan Yin Citta Dharma Door
December 2017

Key Functions of Buddhist Sutras and Mantras for Guan Yin Citta Dharma Door Practitioners

Sutra or Mantra	Key Functions
Great Compassion Mantra	• Fulfil wishes • Strengthen power • Cure illnesses
Heart Sutra	• Calm fluctuating moods and emotions • Gain wisdom
Eighty-Eight Buddhas Great Repentance	• Repent wrongdoings from the past • Eliminate karmic obstacles
Cundi Dharani	• Fulfil wishes (e.g. career, marriage, academic achievement)
Mantra to Untie Karmic Knots	• Resolve interpersonal conflicts (e.g. among couples, colleagues, family • members, etc.)
Xiao Zai Ji Xiang Shen Zhou	• Resolve troubles such as lawsuits, financial loss, sudden illnesses, or impending disasters
Amitabha Pure Land Rebirth Mantra	• Help the spirits of animals (e.g. poultry, seafood and insects) that you may have killed in the past to ascend to a higher spiritual realm
Da Ji Xiang Tian Nü Zhou	• Eliminate poverty, all types of misfortune and attain happiness • Fulfil wishes in a marriage or relationship
Gong De Bao Shan Shen Zhou	• Transform good deeds into merits and virtues • Eliminate karmic obstacles
Qi Fo Mie Zui Zhen Yan	• Eliminate minor karmic obstacles generated recently or during this lifetime
Sheng Wu Liang Shou Jue Ding Guang Ming Wang Tuo Luo Ni	• Extend one's lifespan (especially for the elderly or those suffering from severe illnesses)
Ru Yi Bao Lun Wang Tuo Luo Ni	• Attain success • Receive blessings of Buddha's light
Guan Yin Ling Gan Zhen Yan	• Fulfil wishes quickly

1. Performing Recitations

1.1 Prayers before performing recitations

Guan Yin Bodhisattva can hear the cries of all sentient beings and rescue them from suffering. It is important that you say your prayers to the Greatly Merciful and Greatly Compassionate Guan Yin Bodhisattva and sincerely pray for protection and blessings.

First, you should state your full name. Second, you need to state the issues that you would like Guan Yin Bodhisattva to help you to resolve. For example:

"May the Greatly Merciful and Greatly Compassionate Guan Yin Bodhisattva protect and bless me, <your full name>, grant me good health, help me to eliminate disasters and extend my lifespan, etc."

"May the Greatly Merciful and Greatly Compassionate Guan Yin Bodhisattva protect and bless me, <your full name>, grant me good health, and help me to cure <type of illness>, etc."

"May the Greatly Merciful and Greatly Compassionate Guan Yin Bodhisattva protect and bless me, <your full name>, help me to resolve my negative karmic affinity with <other party's full name>, and resolve our karmic conflicts."

When you say your prayers to Guan Yin Bodhisattva, you must

be sincere and grateful. Say your prayers wholeheartedly. Each time you say your prayers, please limit yourself to one or two wishes. If you have more than three wishes, the effectiveness will be reduced.

1.2 Introduction to reciting sutras and mantras

- Daily recitation is the set of sutras and mantras that one must perform a certain number of every day. For example, a practitioner may recite the **Great Compassion Mantra** 3 times, the **Heart Sutra** 3 times, the **Eighty-Eight Buddhas Great Repentance** once, and the **Amitabha Pure Land Rebirth Mantra** 21 times.

- Performing daily recitation is just as important as our daily food intake, and it is similar to earning an income to cover our daily expenses. Recitation of *Little Houses*, on the other hand, is like paying off your mortgage or other loans. The recitation of sutras and mantras for your daily recitation cannot be counted towards your *Little House* recitation. You also need to make separate prayers for your daily recitation and *Little Houses*. Likewise, the number of recitations of sutras and mantras for your daily recitation should be counted separately from that of *Little Houses*.

- The full title of each sutra and mantra should be recited for each repetition, especially the **Great Compassion Mantra** and the **Heart Sutra**. For example, before reciting the **Great Compassion Mantra**, you should recite its full title, *Qian Shou Qian Yan Wu Ai Da Bei Xin Tuo Luo Ni*. For the **Heart Sutra**, you should recite its full title, *Bo Ruo Bo Luo Mi Duo Xin Jing*.

- It is best to say the corresponding prayers or wishes before you begin your daily recitation. It is recommended that you make no more than three wishes, as making too many wishes would be an act of greed, thus affecting efficacy.

- The **Heart Sutra** and the **Amitabha Pure Land Rebirth Mantra** can be recited until 10pm under good weather conditions. If it is cloudy or rainy, you can recite them during the daytime. However, you should avoid reciting them under extreme weather conditions, such as dark gloomy days, heavy rains, thunderstorms, or lightning. In addition, if you feel weak or uncomfortable when reciting these sutras and mantras, you should recite them during the daytime on a sunny day. Generally speaking, avoid performing any recitations between 2am and 5am.

- If you are performing daily recitation on behalf of family members, friends or fellow Buddhist practitioners, their full names must be announced before you begin reciting in order for the recitation to be effective.

For your reference, brief descriptions of the benefits of some of the sutras and mantras are listed below, as well as the recommended corresponding prayers.

1. The **Great Compassion Mantra** (*Qian Shou Qian Yan Wu Ai Da Bei Xin Tuo Luo Ni*, or *Da Bei Zhou*, *Ta Pei Chou* for short) is one of the fundamental mantras for every Buddhist practitioner and should be included in your daily recitation.

   Some of its functions include fulfilling all the wishes of each sentient being, curing illnesses, and receiving protection and blessings from Dharma Protectors. By

9

reciting this mantra several times a day, you will be able to choose to be reborn into any Buddha Land at the end of your life.

For daily recitation: Generally, 3 or 7 times per day across one's whole life. It can be recited during the day or at night. During critical times such as before and after an operation or being diagnosed with severe illnesses, this mantra should be recited 21 or 49 times per day; the more the better.

Prayer: Before reciting this mantra, you should say the following prayer: "May the Greatly Merciful and Greatly Compassionate Guan Yin Bodhisattva protect and bless me, <your full name>, grant me good health, and strengthen my spiritual power." If you are suffering from an illness, you can also add the following, "May the Greatly Merciful and Greatly Compassionate Guan Yin Bodhisattva cure my illness in <part of your body> and bless me with a speedy recovery."

2. The **Heart Sutra** (*Bo Ruo Bo Luo Mi Duo Xin Jing*, or *Xin Jing*, *Hsin Ching* for short) is for establishing a connection with Guan Yin Bodhisattva and obtaining wisdom through the compassion of Guan Yin Bodhisattva.

This sutra takes the form of power in heaven, currency in the underworld, and wisdom in the human realm.

Some of its functions include disciplining misbehaving children, influencing adults to have a religious belief e.g. Buddhism, making elders less stubborn, calming unstable moods and emotions, granting wisdom, and alleviating depression. It can also be used to help spirits in the underworld ascend to a higher spiritual realm.

For daily recitation: Generally, at least 3 or 7 times per day throughout one's whole life. The *Heart Sutra* can be recited until 10pm during good weather conditions. If it is cloudy or rainy, avoid reciting it after sunset. You should also avoid reciting the sutra during extreme weather conditions including heavy rains, thunderstorms, or lightning.

Prayer: Before reciting this sutra, you should say the following prayer: "May the Greatly Merciful and Greatly Compassionate Guan Yin Bodhisattva protect and bless me, <your full name>, grant me wisdom, calmness and a pure mind, and relieve me of afflictions (maintain focus while performing recitations)."

3. The *Eighty-Eight Buddhas Great Repentance* (*Li Fo Da Chan Hui Wen*) is an important scripture that allows us to repent before Buddhas. By reciting it, we sincerely ask Guan Yin Bodhisattva to help us repent and eliminate karmic obstacles accumulated from our past and present lives.

Some of its functions include repenting the karmic obstacles created in our past and present lives, seeking forgiveness from someone you have hurt in past relationships, resolving long-term karmic conflicts and karmic obstacles, and repenting inappropriate actions such as being disrespectful to Buddhas or Bodhisattvas, or damaging statues or images of Buddhas or Bodhisattvas, etc.

For daily recitation: Generally, 1 to 7 times per day throughout one's whole life. You may recite this scripture both day and night. It is recommended to recite this scripture around 3 times per day. It is best for those who have serious illnesses or heavy karmic obstacles to recite 5 times per day, but no more than 7 times.

Prayer: Before reciting this text, you should say the following prayer: "May the Greatly Merciful and Greatly Compassionate Guan Yin Bodhisattva protect and bless me, <your full name>, help me to repent and eliminate the karmic obstacles (in the body or a specific part of the body), grant me good health and wisdom. "

Note: While reciting the **Eighty-Eight Buddhas Great Repentance**, if you feel soreness or discomfort in any part of your body, it means that the karmic obstacles have been activated and transformed into spirits. This is a good sign, as you can deal with the consequences now rather than having serious illnesses later in life. Generally, you should recite 4 to 7 *Little Houses* or more until you feel better. Those suffering from severe pain or illness should recite additional *Little Houses* until recovery.

The above three sutras and mantras form the foundation of daily recitation. The following sutras and mantras can be recited, depending on your needs, to resolve specific issues.

Generally, they should be recited 21, 27 or 49 times per day.

4. The **Amitabha Pure Land Rebirth Mantra** (*Wang Sheng Jing Tu Shen Zhou*, or *Wang Sheng Zhou* for short) is recited to pray to Guan Yin Bodhisattva to protect and bless us, grant us peace and joy in this life, and allow us to be reborn into the Western Pure Land of Ultimate Bliss in the future. It can also be recited to help the spirits of the animals that you may have killed in the past, including poultry, aquatic creatures, insects, etc. to ascend to a higher spiritual realm.

If you had eaten freshly killed creatures before becoming a Buddhist and starting reciting the Buddhist scriptures, or if you have inadvertently harmed animals, including killing or hurting animals in your dreams, you should recite this mantra.

Recite as necessary: Generally, 21, 27 or 49 times per day. The **Amitabha Pure Land Rebirth Mantra** can be recited until 10pm under good weather conditions. If it is cloudy or rainy, it is recommended that you recite it during the daytime. Avoid reciting the **Amitabha Pure Land Rebirth Mantra** after 10pm, or under extreme weather conditions, including heavy rains, thunderstorms, and lightning.

Prayer: Before reciting this mantra, you should say the following prayer: "May the Greatly Merciful and Greatly Compassionate Guan Yin Bodhisattva protect and bless me, <your full name>, help the spirits of the deceased (animals), whose death my actions caused, ascend to a higher spiritual realm, and help me to eliminate karmic obstacles."

5. The **Mantra to Untie Karmic Knots** (*Jie Jie Zhou*) is to sincerely ask assistance from Guan Yin Bodhisattva to help us resolve interpersonal karmic conflicts.

    Some of its functions include: clearing up misunderstandings in a relationship between couples, fostering harmony in marriage and family, resolving interpersonal conflicts at work, and eliminating karmic obstacles from previous lives.

    Recite as necessary: Generally, 21, 27 or 49 times per day; can be recited during the day or at night.

    Prayer: Before reciting this mantra, you should say the following prayer: "May the Greatly Merciful and Greatly Compassionate Guan Yin Bodhisattva protect and bless me, <your full name>, help me to resolve my negative karmic affinity with <the other party's full name> (can be your relative, friend, or colleague's name)."

6. The **Xiao Zai Ji Xiang Shen Zhou** can be recited when encountering sudden or unexpected situations. It can also be used for resolving karmic conflicts from past lives. Some of its functions include resolving troubles such as lawsuits, financial losses, quarrels, fines and penalties, sudden illnesses, when you have foreseen impending disasters, or when you have nightmares.

<u>Recite as necessary</u>: Generally, 21, 27 or 49 times per day; can be recited during the day or at night.

<u>Prayer</u>: Before reciting this mantra, you should say the following prayer: "May the Greatly Merciful and Greatly Compassionate Guan Yin Bodhisattva protect and bless me, <your full name>, help me to eliminate disasters, and bring me safety and good fortune."

7. The **Cundi Dharani** (*Zhun Ti Shen Zhou*) is used to sincerely ask assistance from Guan Yin Bodhisattva to help us fulfil wishes.

   Some of its functions include praying for success in a career, harmony in marriage and relationships, and academic achievement. It is particularly helpful for young adults looking for a job, a partner in life or hoping to be successful academically. However, the wishes you make must be reasonable and appropriate.

   <u>For daily recitation</u>: Generally, 21, 27 or 49 times per day; can be recited during the day or at night.

   <u>Prayer</u>: Before reciting this mantra, you should say the following prayer: "May the Greatly Merciful and Greatly Compassionate Guan Yin Bodhisattva protect and bless me, <your full name>, help me have my wishes fulfilled and grant me success in career (or any other reasonable wishes you may have)."

8. The **Da Ji Xiang Tian Nü Zhou** can help you to eliminate poverty and all types of misfortune, to obtain prosperity,

happiness, and good fortune in the near future, and to fulfil wishes for your marriage or relationship.

Recitation of the **Da Ji Xiang Tian Nü Zhou** is mainly to pray for good fortune on a specific issue. However, the prerequisite is that you must have accumulated sufficient merits and virtues in order to obtain good or great fortune. If you do not have accumulated enough merits and virtues, then the recitation may not be as effective as expected.

Recite as necessary: Generally, 21, 27 or 49 times per day; can be recited during the day or at night.

Prayer: Before reciting this mantra, you should say the following prayer: "May the Greatly Merciful and Greatly Compassionate Guan Yin Bodhisattva protect and bless me, <your full name>, grant me good fortune and success in <specific issue>."

This mantra can also be used for praying for a good relationship or marriage. In this case, you should say the following prayer: "May the Greatly Merciful and Greatly Compassionate Guan Yin Bodhisattva protect and bless me, <your full name>, help me to find a good partner, and have a good relationship (or marriage)."

9. The **Gong De Bao Shan Shen Zhou** can help you accumulate positive karma, merits and virtues, and eliminate your acts of misconduct and negative karma. Recitation of this mantra can help you to transform your good deeds into merits and virtues. Merits and virtues can be used to eliminate karmic obstacles.

If you have performed many good deeds during a period of time, and you would like to pray for a specific issue, then you can recite the **Gong De Bao Shan Shen Zhou**. For this mantra to be effective, the prerequisite is that you have performed numerous good deeds to serve as a foundation.

Recite as necessary: Generally, 21, 27 or 49 times per day; can be recited during the day or at night.

Prayer: Before reciting this mantra, you should say the following prayer: "May the Greatly Merciful and Greatly Compassionate Guan Yin Bodhisattva protect and bless me, <your full name>, help me to transform the good deeds I have done in the past into merits and virtues, grant me success in <specific issue>."

In addition, you can recite this mantra for an unborn child or a child under 5 years old. Reciting the **Gong De Bao Shan Shen Zhou** helps to transform the child's good deeds from previous lives into merits and virtues in the present life. They can be used to protect and bless the child, help them eliminate disasters, and ensure their safety.

Prayer: Before reciting this mantra for your child, you should say the following prayer: "May the Greatly Merciful and Greatly Compassionate Guan Yin Bodhisattva protect and bless, <full name of your child>, help him/her transform his/her good deeds from the past into merits and virtues, grant the child safety and good health."

For an unborn child, you should say the following prayer: "May the Greatly Merciful and Greatly Compassionate

Guan Yin Bodhisattva protect and bless the child of <your full name>, help him/her transform his/her good deeds from the past into merits and virtues, grant the child safety and good health."

10. The *Qi Fo Mie Zui Zhen Yan* (or *Chi Fo Mieh Tsui Chen Yan*) can help you eliminate karmic obstacles, obtain safety and good fortune, achieve success in every aspect of your life, and benefit future generations.

Recitation of this mantra can help you eliminate relatively minor karmic obstacles that you have generated recently or during this life. For major karmic obstacles or serious ones generated in past lives, you still need to recite the *Eighty-Eight Buddhas Great Repentance*. Therefore, the recitation of the *Qi Fo Mie Zui Zhen Yan* cannot completely replace the recitation of the *Eighty-Eight Buddhas Great Repentance*.

Recite as necessary: For relatively minor negative karma due to actions, speech or thoughts, you can recite this mantra 21, 27 or 49 times in one sitting.

Prayer: Before reciting the *Qi Fo Mie Zui Zhen Yan* you should say the following prayer: "May the Greatly Merciful and Greatly Compassionate Guan Yin Bodhisattva protect and bless me, <your full name>, help me to eliminate karmic obstacles."

In addition, after having performed your daily recitation for a time, you can also recite this mantra 3 times to make yourself purer and cleaner. The minor karmic obstacles that you have generated recently, or on the day of recitation, can be eliminated at the same time. In this case, you do not need to say any prayers before reciting the *Qi Fo Mie Zui Zhen Yan*.

11. The *Sheng Wu Liang Shou Jue Ding Guang Ming Wang Tuo Luo Ni* can help you eliminate the possibility of having a short lifespan or experiencing sudden and unexpected death. It can also help to extend your lifespan, obtain good fortune and quickly realise Bodhi and attain Buddhahood.
    This mantra can be used to extend one's lifespan. It can be used to pray for extending lifespan for elderly people, for those who encounter major predestined calamities, and those who suffer from severe illnesses.

    Recite as necessary: Generally, 21, 27 or 49 times per day; can be recited during the day or at night.

    Prayer: Before reciting this mantra, you should say the following prayer: "May the Greatly Merciful and Greatly Compassionate Guan Yin Bodhisattva protect and bless me, <your full name>, help me to eliminate disasters and extend my lifespan."

12. The *Ru Yi Bao Lun Wang Tuo Luo Ni* can help you receive the blessing of Buddha's light; obtain Buddha's wisdom, extraordinary power and wondrous Dharma; and understand the teachings of Buddha. It can also help you transform your afflictions into Bodhi, be successful in every endeavour, and attain safety and happiness.

Recitation of this mantra is mainly performed to pray for success in a specific issue. For example, praying for success in your career.

Recite as necessary: Generally, 21, 27 or 49 times per day; can be recited during the day or at night.

Prayer: Before reciting this mantra, you should say the following prayer: "May the Greatly Merciful and Greatly Compassionate Guan Yin Bodhisattva protect and bless me, <your full name>, grant me success in <specific issue>."

13. The **Guan Yin Ling Gan Zhen Yan** can help you receive the blessing of Buddha's light, be successful in every aspect of your life, and to obtain good fortune, safety and happiness. Generally, it can be recited to pray to Guan Yin Bodhisattva to perform miracles and grant blessings so that your prayer request will be fulfilled quickly. If afflicted by a sudden or severe illness, you can also recite this mantra to ease the pain.

For this mantra to be effective, the prerequisite is that you must have a pure and clean mind without any distracting thoughts, and sufficient merits and virtues to serve as a foundation. Otherwise, the recitation of this mantra may lead to undesired results. Recitation of this mantra should commence after Master Lu has performed a Totem Reading for you.

Recite as necessary: Generally, 21, 27 or 49 times per day; can be recited during the day or at night.

<u>Prayer</u>: Before reciting this mantra, you should say the following prayer: "May the Greatly Merciful and Greatly Compassionate Guan Yin Bodhisattva protect and bless me, <your full name>, grant me good health, or grant me success in <specific issue>. May Guan Yin Bodhisattva perform miracles."

1.3 Recommendations for daily recitation

1.3.1 Standard daily recitation for beginners

Prayer: "May the Greatly Merciful and Greatly Compassionate Guan Yin Bodhisattva protect and bless me, <your full name>, grant me good health, safety and good fortune."

Recite the *Great Compassion Mantra* 7 times, the *Heart Sutra* 7 times, the *Eighty-Eight Buddhas Great Repentance* 1 to 3 times, and the *Amitabha Pure Land Rebirth Mantra* 21 or 49 times daily.

Prayers for specific situations

1. Praying for success in career, business or interview:
Recite the *Great Compassion Mantra* 7 to 21 times, the *Heart Sutra* 7 to 21 times, the *Eighty-Eight Buddhas Great Repentance* roughly 3 times, the **Cundi Dharani** 21, 49 or 108 times.

2. Praying for resolving karmic conflicts:
Prayer: "May the Greatly Merciful and Greatly Compassionate Guan Yin Bodhisattva protect and bless me, <your full name>, help me to resolve my negative karmic affinity with <other party's full name>."

Recite the *Great Compassion Mantra* 7 times, the *Heart Sutra* 7, 9, 11, 21, 27 or 49 times each for yourself and the other party, the *Eighty-Eight Buddhas Great Repentance* 3 times, and the **Mantra to Untie Karmic Knots** 21, 27, 49 or 108 times. In addition, you should recite at least 3 *Little Houses* (addressed to your karmic creditor) per week, combined with making great vows and performing life liberations. The above will help to resolve the negative karmic affinity between the two parties as soon as possible.

If the negative karmic affinity between the two parties is very deep, you can resolve this karmic conflict by reciting *Little Houses*, addressing them to "<Your full name> resolves karmic conflicts". As you say your prayers, you may say both parties' names. For example: "May the Greatly Merciful and Greatly Compassionate Guan Yin Bodhisattva help me, <your full name>, to resolve my negative karmic affinity with my husband <full name of your husband>." You may recite 7 *Little Houses* as the first batch, and then continue with 7 *Little Houses* for every subsequent batch.

While reciting *Little Houses* for resolving karmic conflicts, you should not stop reciting *Little Houses* for your karmic creditors, as one cannot replace the other. The *Little Houses* for resolving karmic conflict can help resolve negative karmic affinities in a powerful way, however, karmic creditors will not receive these *Little Houses*. Hence, you still need to recite *Little Houses* for your karmic creditors to repay the karmic debts accumulated from past lives.

1.3.2 Daily recitation for elders

Prayer: "May the Greatly Merciful and Greatly Compassionate Guan Yin Bodhisattva protect and bless me, <your full name>, grant me good health, and help me eliminate disasters and extend my lifespan."

Recite the **Great Compassion Mantra** 21 to 49 times, the **Heart Sutra** 7 to 21 times, the **Eighty-Eight Buddhas Great Repentance** roughly 3 times, the **Amitabha Pure Land Rebirth Mantra** 21 or 49 times, the **Sheng Wu Liang Shou Jue Ding Guang Ming Wang Tuo Luo Ni** 49 times, and the **Amitabha Sutra** 3 to 7 times. You may recite this scripture if you wish to ascend to the Western Pure Land of Ultimate Bliss, it is best to recite this after the age of 60 or 70 years.

1.3.3 Daily recitation for people with severe illness

In general, if you have discovered that you have cancer, this means that your karmic obstacles have already broken out. At such times, it is best not to recite the **Great Compassion Mantra** too many times; you can recite it 21 times per day. You should do more recitations of the **Heart Sutra**, e.g. 49 times per day.

Once your condition becomes stable, you can increase your recitations of the **Great Compassionate Mantra** to 49 times per day. You should continue to recite the **Heart Sutra** 49 times daily.

During critical periods or before surgery, you should focus on reciting the **Great Compassionate Mantra** and say the following prayer: "May the Greatly Merciful and Greatly Compassionate Guan Yin Bodhisattva protect and bless me, <your full name>, grant me good health and cure my illness in <part of body> soon."

It is important for people with cancer to persist with the recitation of the **Great Compassionate Mantra** for the rest of their lives.

For people suffering from mental illness, avoid reciting the **Great Compassionate Mantra** too many times, restricting themselves to 21 times or fewer per day. However, they should do more recitations of the **Heart Sutra**, usually 21 or 49 times per day.

You should recite the **Eighty-Eight Buddhas Great Repentance** 3 to 5 times per day to repent of your karmic obstacles. According to the message passed on to Master Lu by Guan Yin Bodhisattva, recitation of **the Eighty-Eight Buddhas Great Repentance** is very effective for curing cancer and acute diseases. The **Eighty-Eight Buddhas Great Repentance** can both eliminate and activate karmic obstacles. Hence, to ensure good results it must be combined with the recitation of *Little Houses*. Generally, if you recite the **Eighty-Eight Buddhas Great Repentance** 3 to 5 times per day, you will need to give at least 3 to 5 *Little Houses* per week to your karmic creditors. Provided they can maintain a certain number of *Little Houses* each week, those suffering serious illnesses can recite the **Eighty-Eight Buddhas Great Repentance** 5 times per day.

If you have committed karma of killing (of various animals) in this life, or your ancestors had karma of killing, you should recite the **Amitabha Pure Land Rebirth Mantra** 27 or 49 times per day in order to help the spirits of the deceased, whose death your actions caused, ascend to a higher spiritual realm.

You need to recite and burn at least 3 *Little Houses* per week. However, it is better to recite as many as you can. It would be best to make a vow and state the number of *Little Houses* you will recite in a single batch. For example, you could vow to recite 21 or 49 *Little Houses* before a certain date. After finishing the batch, you can continue reciting *Little Houses* in similar batches until you have recovered. In addition, whenever you finish reciting 3 to 4 *Little Houses,* you should burn them as soon as you can. Do not wait until you have completed the full number of *Little Houses* pledged before burning them.

If you have dreams about deceased family members or have previously had an abortion or miscarriage, you should help the deceased and the aborted/miscarried child to ascend to a higher spiritual realm as soon as possible. Generally, you need to recite and burn at least 7 *Little Houses* for an aborted and miscarried child (Address them to "Child of <full name of the mother>") or a deceased family member (Address them to <full name of the deceased>). It would be best if they can recite more than 21 *Little Houses*.

Meanwhile, it is recommended that you make vows. The greater the vow, the greater the effectiveness, but you must keep your vow. For example: "If I recover, I will introduce

Buddhism to <number of> people, helping them become spiritually awakened," or "If I recover, I will share my experience with others to demonstrate the benefits of practising Buddhism."

If you think your abilities are limited, you can make such vows as: "For the rest of my life, I will adopt a vegetarian diet on the 1st and 15th day of the lunar month," "For the rest of my life, I will not eat freshly killed seafood or other creatures," "For the rest of my life, I will not perform the act of killing," etc.

At the same time, you should perform life liberations frequently, preferably in large quantities. For best results, you can perform life liberations on the 1st and 15th day of each lunar month. When you arrive at the site of life liberation, you can recite the *Great Compassionate Mantra, the Heart Sutra* and the *Amitabha Pure Land Rebirth Mantra*. There is no limit to the number of recitations that you can do, but the more the better. Before reciting those sutras and mantras, you should state your full name and say the following prayer: "May the Greatly Merciful and Greatly Compassionate Guan Yin Bodhisattva protect and bless me, <your full name>, grant me good health and cure my illness in <part of body>."

If it is inconvenient for you to perform the life liberation yourself, you can ask your family members to do it on your behalf. For best results, the patient should use their own money for the life liberations.

Performing recitations, making vows, and performing life liberations are the Three Golden Buddhist Practices that the

Greatly Merciful and Greatly Compassionate Guan Yin Bodhisattva bestows upon us to cure illnesses. We must learn to use them wisely and skilfully.

2. Repaying Karmic Debts by Reciting *Little Houses*

From the Buddhist point of view, there are two kinds of illness. One is caused by your physical body itself, and the other is caused by foreign spirits. Spirits and ghosts are commonly associated with the spirit world. Foreign spirits that occupy a living person are usually deceased relatives, aborted or miscarried children, deceased close friends or foes, and foreign spirit(s) from their houses. If foreign spirits occupy a person's body for an extended period of time, this person can experience physical illness, bad temper, misfortune, and difficulty in career or studies.

Buddhist Master Jun Hong Lu, an Australia-based Chinese Buddhist cultivator, has obtained transcendental abilities thanks to the blessings of Buddhas and Bodhisattvas. Under the guidance of Guan Yin Bodhisattva, Master Jun Hong Lu gives people advice on how to change their lives for the better, be free of suffering, and attain happiness. He teaches people to recite sutras and mantras, as well as *Little Houses*, to help spirits ascend to a higher spiritual realm so that they can recover from the illnesses caused by foreign spirits. The *Little House* (a sample can be found in **Appendix A**) can also be used to help deceased relatives ascend to higher spiritual realms, including heaven.

The *Little House* is one of the valuable methods the Greatly

Merciful and Greatly Compassionate Guan Yin Bodhisattva bestows upon us to help spirits ascend to a higher spiritual realm and to eliminate our karmic obstacles in this Age of Dharma Decline.

In the spirit world, the *Little House* is like a high value cheque. By way of the recitation of *Little Houses*, we are able to repay karmic debts from previous lives. They provide spirits, including deceased loved ones, with the power to ascend to a higher spiritual realm. Therefore, the *Little House* is a great tool for helping ourselves as well as others. It works miracles!

For more details, please refer to another of Master Jun Hong Lu's publications: *A Guide to Reciting the Combination of Buddhist Scriptures: Little Houses.*

2.1 Examples of how to fill out *Little Houses*

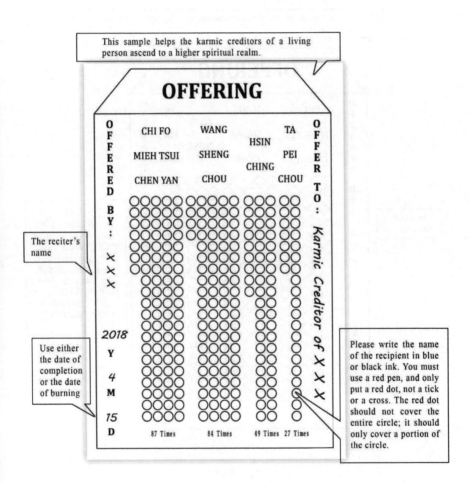

This sample helps the karmic creditors of a living person ascend to a higher spiritual realm.

OFFERING

OFFERED BY:

CHI FO   WANG   TA
                 HSIN
MIEH TSUI   SHENG   PEI
                 CHING
CHEN YAN   CHOU   CHOU

The reciter's name

× × ×

2018 Y

4 M

15 D

OFFER TO: *Karmic Creditor of* XXX

Use either the date of completion or the date of burning

87 Times   84 Times   49 Times 27 Times

Please write the name of the recipient in blue or black ink. You must use a red pen, and only put a red dot, not a tick or a cross. The red dot should not cover the entire circle; it should only cover a portion of the circle.

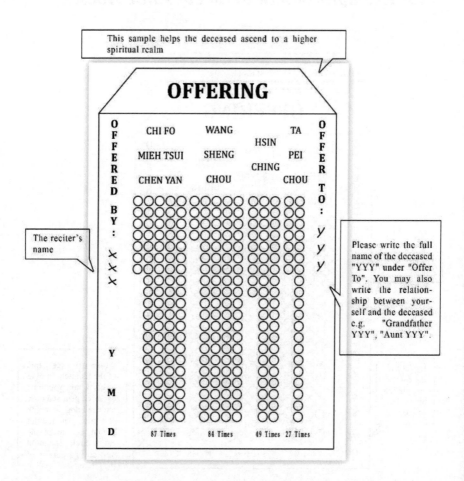

This sample helps the deceased ascend to a higher spiritual realm

OFFERING

OFFERED BY:

CHI FO   WANG   TA
                HSIN
MIEH TSUI SHENG   PEI
               CHING
CHEN YAN   CHOU   CHOU

OFFER TO:

The reciter's name

87 Times   84 Times   49 Times 27 Times

Please write the full name of the deceased "YYY" under "Offer To". You may also write the relationship between yourself and the deceased e.g. "Grandfather YYY", "Aunt YYY".

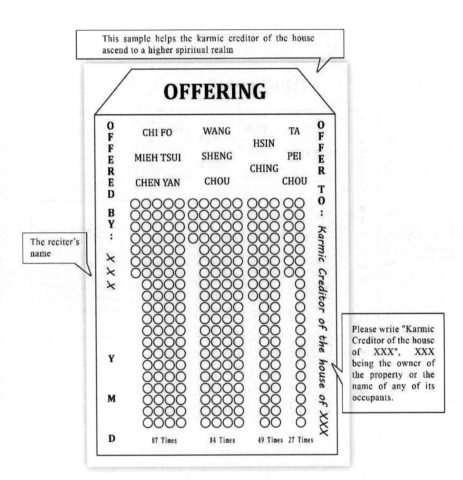

This sample helps the karmic creditor of the house ascend to a higher spiritual realm

OFFERING

O F F E R E D B Y : X X X

OFFERED TO : *Karmic Creditor of the house of XXX*

CHI FO   WANG   TA

HSIN

MIEH TSUI   SHENG   PEI

CHING

CHEN YAN   CHOU   CHOU

Y M D

87 Times   84 Times   49 Times   27 Times

The reciter's name

Please write "Karmic Creditor of the house of XXX", XXX being the owner of the property or the name of any of its occupants.

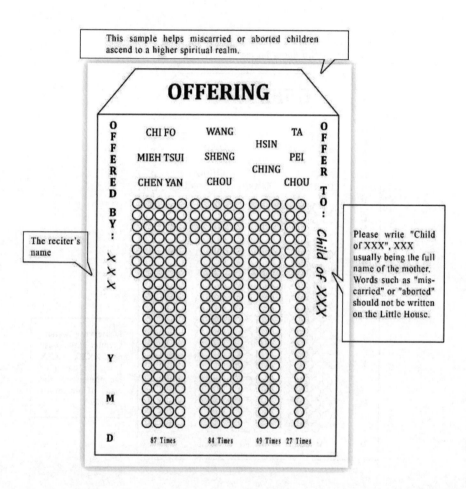

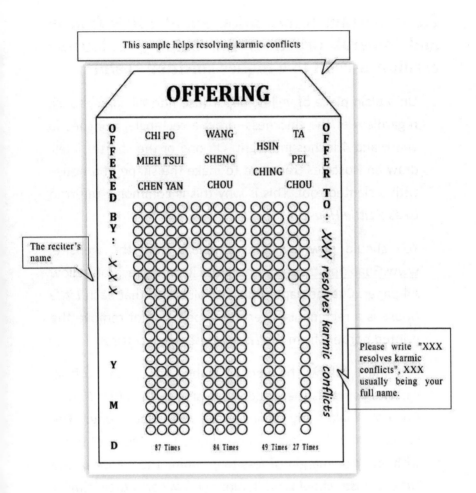

2.2 Important information about *Little Houses* and general practices for helping a karmic creditor ascend to a higher spiritual realm

1. On a plain piece of yellow paper (use normal copy paper), regardless of the thickness, draw a rectangle, 3 inches in width and 4 inches in height. On one of the shorter lines, draw an isosceles trapezoid to make the shape of a house with a slanted roof. This is why this is commonly referred to as a *Little House*.

    You should download the template from the website, www.GuanYinCitta.com, and print it on a piece of yellow A4 paper. Cut the paper into four pieces so that each *Little House* is a rectangular piece of paper. Do not remove the printed borders from the *Little House* when cutting.

    You must follow the version published on the official website as this is the standard version of the *Little House*. Do not make any changes to the typesetting. The dimension of the black borders should be 9.1cm x 13.95cm, with an error margin of less than 5mm. The colour of the *Little House* should be lemon yellow or other similar shades of yellow.

2. The *"Little House"* consists of a combination of sutras and mantras. It consists of the **Great Compassion Mantra** (to be recited 27 times), the **Heart Sutra** (to be recited 49 times), the **Amitabha Pure Land Rebirth Mantra** (to be

recited 84 times), and the **Qi Fo Mie Zui Zhen Yan** (to be recited 87 times). The number that you recite should not be fewer than the required number. It is fine if you recite more than required, but do not recite it excessively.

3. The **Great Compassion Mantra** and the **Qi Fo Mie Zui Zhen Yan** can be recited any time at any place. The **Heart Sutra** and the **Amitabha Pure Land Rebirth Mantra** can be recited until 10pm under good weather conditions. If it is cloudy or rainy, you can recite them during the daytime. If you are in the countryside, in a car, or in a crowd, you should be extra careful, and recite them quietly. It is best to avoid reciting them after 10pm. Nevertheless, if you have filled in the "Offer To" field, you may recite them until 12am. Furthermore, avoid reciting them under extreme weather conditions, such as dark gloomy days, heavy rains, thunderstorms, or lightning. In addition, if you feel weak or uncomfortable when reciting these sutras and mantras, then you should try to recite them during the daytime on a sunny day.

4. Each time before you recite a *Little House*, you can recite the **Great Compassion Mantra** several times to enhance your spiritual power. This will make your recitation of the *Little House* more effective. It is best to avoid reciting the *Little House* when you are feeling unwell or emotionally unstable. This is because reciting the *Little House* consumes energy. If you cannot maintain focus, it will not be as effective.

However, if these symptoms are caused by spirits, you should recite *Little Houses* to help them to ascend to a higher spiritual realm as soon as possible. When you feel tired or feel discomfort in parts of your body during recitation, you can stop reciting the *Little House* and recite the **Great Compassion Mantra** instead to enhance your own spiritual power before continuing your *Little House* recitation. If you are so keen to help the spirit ascend to a higher spiritual realm that your lips begin to have sores and blisters due to recitation, this is a sign that you are stretching beyond your limits. This is not permissible.

The four scriptures in the *Little House* can be recited in any order. You may observe the following order if you prefer: start and end the recitation of the *Little House* with **the Great Compassion Mantra**; recite the **Great Compassion Mantra** before commencing the recitation of each of the other three scriptures. For example:

o   Start by reciting the **Great Compassion Mantra** 9 times;

o   Follow this with the **Great Compassion Mantra** 3 times and the **Heart Sutra** 49 times;

o   This should then be followed by the **Great Compassion Mantra** 3 times and the **Amitabha Pure Land Rebirth Mantra** 84 times;

o   Continue to the **Great Compassion Mantra** 3 times and the **Qi Fo Mie Zui Zhen Yan** 87 times;

o   Complete your recitation with the **Great Compassion Mantra** 9 times.

Using this approach will make the *Little House* very powerful. As the **Great Compassion Mantra** envelops the other scriptures, it not only enhances their power but also safeguards them.

5. On the upper right-hand side of the *Little House*, write the name of the recipient in blue or black ink. If it is to be offered to your karmic creditor, address it to the "Karmic Creditor of <your full name>". If it is to be offered to a child that was aborted or miscarried, address it to "Child of <full name of the mother>". If it is to be offered to a deceased relative or friend, address it to "<full name of the deceased>". You may also write the relationship between yourself and the deceased e.g. "Grandfather XXX". If your purpose is to resolve karmic conflicts, you may address it to "<Your full name> resolves karmic conflicts".

The "Offered by" (the reciter) field on the left-hand side of the *Little House* must be filled in with a blue or black pen by the person who is going to recite; the name must be that of the reciter. This field should be completed prior to commencing recitations and filling in the red dots. Otherwise, the power from the recitation can be easily lost. The Date field on the left-hand side must only be filled in after the *Little House* has been completed. The date can be the day you complete the recitations or the day of burning the *Little House*.

The sutras and mantras must be recited before the red dots are added; dots must not be added before the recitations are completed. Each time you finish reciting a sutra or mantra, use a red marker to fill the corresponding circle. Alternatively, you can add the dots after reciting a series or an entire section of sutras and mantras. The number of sutras and mantras recited can exceed the number of circles on the *Little Houses* but must not fall short of the required number.

Do not tick, cross, or dot outside the edge of the circle or fill the circle right to its rim. You are only allowed to fill red dots. When adding the red dots, it is best to start from the bottom, moving towards the top of the *Little House*. You can add dots for each individual section of sutras and mantras, or you can add dots across all four sutras and mantras from the bottom to the top. This is like building the foundation for a house. The house will be more stable with a solid foundation.

6. Before you recite the *Little House*, you can say your prayer as follows, "May the Greatly Merciful and Greatly Compassionate Guan Yin Bodhisattva protect and bless me, <your full name>, help me to give these <number> *Little Houses* to XXX (being the recipient of the *Little House* that is written under "Offer To:" on the right-hand side, i.e. Karmic Creditor of <your full name>, Child of <mother's full name>, <full name of the deceased>, Karmic Creditor of the house of <full name of the occupant>)." For a *Little House* used to resolve karmic conflicts, say, "May the Greatly Merciful and Greatly Compassionate Guan Yin Bodhisattva protect and bless me, <your full name>, help

me to resolve my negative karmic affinity with <the other party's full name>. (Note that "the other party" can be your relative, friend, or colleague.) Generally, only your name will appear on the *Little House* and not the name of the other party.

Generally, beginners can recite 4 to 10 *Little Houses* and address them to the "Karmic Creditor of <your full name>". If you have previously had an abortion, miscarriage, or ectopic pregnancy, you need to recite at least 7 *Little Houses* for each child (it is best to recite 21 or more *Little Houses*). If the child was destined to claim karmic debts from you, you may need to offer more *Little Houses*. After having burnt the *Little Houses*, if you dream about a child dressed beautifully and leaving happily, or being led away by someone else, it means that the child has left. Conversely, if you dream about a child in an unfavourable condition, you have to offer more *Little Houses* to help the child ascend to a higher spiritual realm. If you dream about the deceased, you will need to recite at least 7 *Little Houses* for each of the deceased you dream about. Generally, you should offer 21 *Little Houses* or more if the deceased is a relative.

7. Generally, you should use the name that is on your birth certificate. However, if you have changed your name for over one year, it is likely that your new name has become active spiritually. To err on the side of caution, it would be best to lodge the *Application for Change of Name* after you have changed your name. After that, you can use your new

name when you recite *Little Houses*. However, after you lodge the *Application for Change of Name*, you do not need to change your name on your ID card, passport, driver's license, etc.

8. Find a suitable time and a quiet place at home to perform recitations and avoid interruptions such as calls, visitors, etc. If you are interrupted while reciting a long sutra, you should excuse yourself by reciting *"Ong Lai Mu Suo He"* once to pause your recitation. Once you have finished attending to the tasks that interrupted you, you may resume your recitation by reciting *"Ong Lai Mu Suo He"* once again. For short mantras, it is best to start over.

9. You can perform recitations aloud or silently. However, if you recite too loud, you will hurt your *Qi*, or energy flow. On the other hand, if you recite completely in silence, your blood circulation will be affected. The best method is to recite softly. The full title of each sutra and mantra should be recited each time before you recite the sutra and mantra. For example, before reciting the **Great Compassion Mantra** and the **Heart Sutra**, you should recite the full title: **Qian Shou Qian Yan Wu Ai Da Bei Xin Tuo Luo Ni** and **Bo Ruo Bo Luo Mi Duo Xin Jing** respectively. Some slight pronunciation variations are acceptable, as long as they are not too far from the correct pronunciation. You can recite the **Mantra for Rectifying Errors in Recitation** 3 to 7 times at the end of your recitation. English speakers can recite the sutras and mantras

according to the Wade-Giles Romanization or Hanyu Pinyin and achieve the same effects. It is best if you can recite the sutras and mantras from memory, but do not leave out the words and phrases.

10. For a *Little House*, you do not need to finish reciting all four sutras and mantras in one day. While there are no specific requirements regarding the time period needed to complete the recitation of a *Little House*, you should avoid prolonged delays.

    Fill in the completion date (according to the Gregorian calendar) once you have finished, and you can burn it on the day or a later day. If you are not burning it on the day, keep it in a red envelope or wrap it with red coloured materials (e.g. red paper or red fabrics) to prevent its energy from being dissipated.

11. When you are burning *Little Houses* and you have an altar at home, you can use an oil lamp, lighter, or matches to burn it. But generally, avoid using the oil lamp on your altar to light it. If you do not have an altar at home, you may use a lighter or matches. It is best to burn the *Little House* from the upper right-hand corner where it says "Offer To", or burn it from bottom to top. If the karmic creditor is very eager to obtain the *Little House*, you should burn it from the corner where it says "Offer To". Under normal circumstances, you may also burn them from bottom to top. You should burn the *Little House* in a white bowl or plate made from ceramics, such as china and

porcelain. Metal and alloy containers should not be used. The bowl or plate used for burning the *Little House* should not be placed on the altar or directly on the floor. You can place a wooden plank or a small stool designated for burning *Little House* in front of the altar. Do not hold the *Little House* with your hands, instead, you can use tweezers or chopsticks (metal ones are acceptable) to hold the *Little House* and burn it. Ensure that the entire piece of paper is thoroughly burnt, and then you can wrap the ashes up and discard them. Please note that you should not flush the ashes down the toilet or scatter the ashes in the open. For your dedicated white bowl or plate, you can clean it and use it again next time.

12. The best times to burn *Little Houses* are 8am, 10am and 4pm. Any other time during daytime on a sunny day is also alright. Generally, the period between 6am and sunset is suitable for burning *Little Houses* if the weather is good. Do not burn them after sunset, or on a cloudy and rainy day, unless it is urgent, for example, if the Karmic Creditor is being very demanding, or during times of severe illness, etc.

13. If you have an altar at home, you must make incense offerings before you burn *Little Houses*. First of all, you should make incense offerings, and then make prostrations and say, "I express my sincere gratitude to the Greatly Merciful and Greatly Compassionate Guan Yin Bodhisattva" three times. Raise the *Little Houses* slightly above your

head, and then place them on your altar. Kneel down and say the following prayer: "May the Greatly Merciful and Greatly Compassionate Guan Yin Bodhisattva protect and bless me, <your full name>, help me give the *Little Houses* to <name of the recipient>". The name can be your karmic creditor, name of a deceased person, an aborted or miscarried child, or the karmic creditor of someone's house.

When you are burning *Little Houses* (it is best to burn from top to bottom, starting from the upper right-hand corner where it says "Offer To"), you can say the following prayer, "May the Greatly Merciful and Greatly Compassionate Guan Yin Bodhisattva protect and bless me with your compassion." You can then light the *Little Houses*. While you are burning *Little Houses*, please do not recite or say anything extra. Simply say, "May the Greatly Merciful and Greatly Compassionate Guan Yin Bodhisattva protect and bless me with your compassion."

After you finish burning *Little Houses*, you can say the following, "I bow in gratitude to the Greatly Merciful and Greatly Compassionate Guan Yin Bodhisattva for helping me give these *Little Houses* to <name of the recipient>. I express my deepest gratitude to the Greatly Merciful and Greatly Compassionate Guan Yin Bodhisattva for protecting and blessing me." (with one full prostration). You could also say corresponding prayers. For example, if you give *Little Houses* to the karmic creditor of <someone's full name>, you could pray to Guan Yin Bodhisattva to grant this person good health, safety and good fortune. If you use a *Little House* to resolve X's karmic conflicts, you could pray to Guan Yin Bodhisattva to help resolve the negative karmic affinity between X and Y.

If you do not have an altar at home, you can burn *Little Houses* on your balcony, near the window in your living room, or in your backyard. You should offer Heart Incense[1] and say, "I express my sincere gratitude to the Greatly Merciful and Greatly Compassionate Guan Yin Bodhisattva" three times. You can then recite the **Great Compassion Mantra** once and the **Heart Sutra** once. After that, raise the *Little Houses* slightly above your head and bow three times facing a direction that you can see the sky, or visualise yourself kneeling down and say the following prayer: "May the Greatly Merciful and Greatly Compassionate Guan Yin Bodhisattva protect and bless me, <your full name>, help me give these *Little Houses* to <name of the recipient>"; the recipient can be your karmic creditor, a deceased person, an aborted or miscarried child, or the karmic creditor of someone's house. Finally, you can burn the *Little Houses*. The procedure to be followed after burning the *Little Houses* is the same as described above.

14. Family members who believe in Buddhism can burn *Little Houses* on your behalf. If you want to help your karmic creditor ascend to a higher spiritual realm, the family member who will burn the *Little House* on your behalf can

---

[1] *Please refer to Q&A 094: Difference between offering Heart Incense and real incense in Buddhism: Your Questions Answered.*

say the following, "May the Greatly Merciful and Greatly Compassionate Guan Yin Bodhisattva help <name of the reciter> to give the *Little Houses* to his/her karmic creditor."

15. If you are reciting *Little Houses* for someone else to cure their illness, it is possible that the spirit that is currently occupying their body will come and occupy your body instead. It is best to include the following prayer before you recite the *Little Houses*, "May the Greatly Merciful and Greatly Compassionate Guan Yin Bodhisattva protect and bless me, <your full name>, I will recite <number of> *Little Houses* for <full name of your relative or friend>. May <Full name of your relative or friend>'s karmic creditor please ask <full name of your relative or friend> for the remaining *Little Houses*."

Alternatively, you can fill in the reciter field on the *Little House*, and leave the recipient field blank. The *Little Houses* can be accumulated and then given to those in need. This is the recommended method. Note that you do not need to specify to whom these *Little Houses* are addressed before reciting.

In the event that the other party's Karmic Creditor comes to you, it is best to recite several *Little Houses* and address them to the "Karmic Creditor of <your full name>". It is a meritorious deed to save others, but saving people often involves generosity and sacrifice.

16. When conditions allow, you can reserve *Little Houses* for future use. As soon as any issues arise, you can immediately burn these *Little Houses* to resolve the problem. Before you recite the *Little House*, simply say the following prayer: "May the Greatly Merciful and Greatly Compassionate Guan Yin Bodhisattva be my witness, I, <your full name>, now recite the scriptures contained in this *Little House* (the **Great Compassion Mantra**, the **Heart Sutra**, the **Amitabha Pure Land Rebirth Mantra**, and the **Qi Fo Mie Zui Zhen Yan**)." Leave the recipient field and date blank until you are going to burn the *Little Houses*. Preserve the *Little Houses* that you have recited by wrapping them with red paper or red fabric.

17. If you make a mistake when you fill in the details for the *Little House*, you can re-dot the sutras and mantras that you have recited and re-write the details onto a new *Little House*. After that, use a pen to cross out the name written in the "Offer to" and "Offered by" fields, fold the mistaken *Little House* several times into a small piece of paper, and then wrap it with a piece of paper before discarding it (Do not tear the old *Little House* nor burn it). You can say the following, "Namo the Greatly Merciful and Greatly Compassionate Guan Yin Bodhisattva, I, <your full name>, have made a mistake on this *Little House* and it is now invalid."

18. When you recite *Little Houses* for the deceased to help them ascend to a higher spiritual realm, it is best not to

burn joss paper, spirit money, or other joss materials at the same time. Even though burning *Little Houses* and burning spirit money are both considered to be offering money to the deceased, *Little Houses* are deemed to be the largest denomination of banknote in the underworld, and a form of energy in heaven, while spirit money is only considered as coins and can only be used in the underworld. If the deceased are currently in the underworld, they can receive both spirit money and *Little Houses*. However, if the deceased are in the *Asura* realm or heaven, then the burning of joss material may cause them to fall to the lower realms. It is because the foundations of the deceased family members ascended to the realm of *Asura* or heaven are not stable. Their ascension is due to the energy from the *Little Houses* that we have recited and burnt for them, rather than the efforts from their own. When they see spirit money being burnt for them, they tend to be greedy and come down to get the money. This is why they fall. Therefore, it is best to ask family members to recite more *Little Houses* together. If you are unable to convince them, the only way is to recite more *Little Houses*. That way, even if other people are burning spirit money, as long as you offer more banknotes (*Little Houses*), the deceased would not care for the coins (spirit money). Every time you burn the *Little Houses*, you can say the following prayer: "May the Greatly Merciful and Greatly Compassionate Guan Yin Bodhisattva protect and bless <full name of the deceased person>, help him/her to proceed to a higher realm using the power from *Little*

Houses, and not be greedy and become attached to the low-value currencies from the human realm."

19. Please note that the recitations of *Little Houses* to help karmic creditors ascend to a higher spiritual realm are a life-long endeavour, and it does not mean that after you have recited and burnt a certain number of *Little Houses*, you would never need to recite any more. After you have finished reciting your current batch of *Little Houses*, it merely means that you have successfully helped the current spirit ascend to a higher spiritual realm. Over time, a portion of your karmic obstacles will be activated and transformed into spirits or you may accidentally invite other spirits to occupy your body. This may be due to having a fight with someone or visiting the cemetery, hospital, or crematorium, etc. Therefore, you should continuously perform recitations of *Little Houses* according to different circumstances.

20. Below are typical situations where *Little Houses* are needed, together with the recommended number of *Little Houses*.

   a. You experience pain in a particular part of the body, for example, the lower back, shoulders, etc, which cannot be diagnosed by doctors as test results show that everything is normal. Generally, this is an illness caused by spirits. You may recite 7 to 9 *Little Houses* first, addressing them to the "Karmic Creditor of <your full name>". If it is insufficient, you may continue reciting *Little Houses* until you fully recover.

b. Cancer patients usually have powerful foreign spirits occupying their body. This is a form of serious karmic retribution. You may recite the **Heart Sutra** 49 times, **Great Compassion Mantra** 21 times, and the **Eighty-Eight Buddhas Great Repentance** 5 times per day. Meanwhile, you should also recite as many *Little Houses* as possible. Reciting *Little Houses* can save your life by repaying karmic debts. For the first batch, you need at least 49 *Little Houses*, and you should continue your recitations until your condition stabilises. Meanwhile, you should also perform life liberations and make great vows.

c. If you often lose your temper for no apparent reason, generally you need to recite 7 or more *Little Houses*. Address the *Little Houses* to the "Karmic Creditor of <your full name>".

d. For helping the spirits of the aborted or miscarried children ascend to a higher spiritual realm, you need to recite 7 to 21 *Little Houses* for each child. Address the *Little Houses* to the "Child of <full name of the mother>". You may need to recite more *Little Houses* if they are here to claim their karmic debts from you.

e. If you have a headache or fever, generally you need to recite 7 or more *Little Houses*. Address the *Little Houses* to the "Karmic Creditor of <your full name>".

f. If there are strange sounds in your house, your

electrical appliances unexpectedly malfunction, or your sewage pipes are constantly clogged, generally you need to recite 4 to 7 *Little Houses* to help the foreign spirits in your house ascend to a higher spiritual realm. Address the *Little Houses* to the "Karmic Creditor of the house of <full name of the occupant>". The occupant can be the owner of the house, or the person living in the house. If you are renting, you can address it to the Karmic Creditor of the house of <your full name>.

g. Regarding helping your deceased relatives to ascend to a higher spiritual realm, you need to recite at least 49 *Little Houses* within the 49 days immediately after the death of each relative. Address the *Little Houses* to <full name of the deceased>.

h. If you dream about a deceased person, for example, your relatives or parents, you need to recite at least 7 *Little Houses* for each relative. If you know the full name of the deceased, you should address the *Little Houses* to <full name of the deceased>. Generally, when you recite *Little Houses* to help the spirit of the deceased ascend to a higher spiritual realm, you need at least 21 *Little Houses* to help them to proceed to the next higher realm. For example, if the deceased person is in the underworld, you would need to recite 21 *Little Houses* for them to be able to be reborn into the human realm, and an additional 21 *Little Houses* for him to be able to be reborn into the *Asura* realm, and then another 21 *Little Houses* for them to be able to be reborn into heaven. If you dream of an unfamiliar person who is dressed in black, you need to recite 4 *Little Houses* for each person, and address them to the "Karmic Creditor of <your full name>".

i. Reciting the **Eighty-Eight Buddhas Great Repentance** may result in your karmic obstacles being activated and transformed into spirits, so you need to recite *Little Houses*. For example, if you recite the **Eighty-Eight Buddhas Great Repentance** 3 times per day, you need to recite 3 or more *Little Houses* per week. If you recite the **Eighty-Eight Buddhas Great Repentance** 5 times per day, you need to recite 5 or more *Little Houses* per week.

21. To determine if you have successfully helped the spirits to ascend to a higher spiritual realm, please try calling into Master Lu's radio program every Tuesday, Thursday and Saturday, 5-6pm Sydney, Australian time. The phone number is +61 2 96988866. You can speak directly to Master Lu and sincerely ask him to perform a Totem Reading for you. However, since practitioners all over the world are trying to call into the program, it may be difficult to get through. Therefore, the following can be referenced as guidelines:

a. If you are helping a spirit that is occupying a particular part of the body to ascend to a higher spiritual realm, you have burnt a sufficient number of *Little Houses*, and you no longer feel pain in this part of the body, that means you have successfully helped the spirit to ascend to a higher spiritual realm.

b. If you are helping a spirit of an aborted or miscarried child to ascend to a higher spiritual realm, once you have burnt a sufficient number of *Little Houses* you will dream about a well-dressed child visiting you with a smiling face. This means that you have successfully helped the spirit ascend to a higher spiritual realm.

c. If you are helping the spirits of your ancestors, relatives or friends to ascend to a higher spiritual realm, once you have burnt a sufficient number of *Little Houses*, and in your dream, they are dressed neatly and visiting you in a bright environment, then it means that they have ascended to the *Asura* realm or heaven.

d. If you are helping the foreign spirit that is occupying your house to ascend to a higher spiritual realm, once you have burnt a sufficient number of *Little Houses*, and there are no more strange sounds in your house and you also feel comfortable at home, it means you have successfully helped the spirit to ascend to a higher spiritual realm.

22. The above method for helping spirits to ascend to a higher spiritual realm is applicable to all deceased persons. If you wish to help the spirits of animals to ascend a higher spiritual realm, you should recite the **Amitabha Pure Land Rebirth Mantra**. For example, you can recite it 108 times

for a cow; 49 times for a pig, sheep or mouse; 7 times for a fish, crab or chicken; 3 times for a shrimp or prawn; and once for a mosquito or an ant.

3. Performing Life Liberation

1. What are the merits that can be accrued from performing life liberations? The performing of life liberations encompasses all three types of giving: the giving of wealth, the giving of Dharma, and the giving of fearlessness. Hence, it can help us accumulate immeasurable merits and virtues. The greatest benefits that we can receive from performing life liberations are quelling disasters and extending our lifespan. When we seek the mercy of the Greatly Merciful and Greatly Compassionate Guan Yin Bodhisattva for protection and blessings in the event of major incidents, better results will be achieved if life liberation is performed in addition to reciting Buddhist scriptures.

2. Individuals who need to perform life liberation in particular include Buddhist devotees, senior and middle-aged people, elders with health problems, and people showing filial piety to their parents. People in the following occupations should also perform life liberation: kitchen staff, chefs, surgeons, doctors who perform abortions, funeral and burial workers, pesticide and sanitation workers, animal farm butchers, police officers, forensic and medical examiners who perform post mortems, etc. People in these occupations should frequently perform life liberation to eliminate their misdeeds and negative karma. It would, however, be best to seek opportunities to change careers altogether.

3. In regard to the timing of performing life liberation, any time throughout the year is suitable. For people who would like to pray for longevity, it is best to perform life liberations on their birthday. Other significant dates include Chinese New Year's Eve, the transitional period between the old and new years, the 1st and 15th of each lunar month, and the birthdays of Buddhas and Bodhisattvas. Other suitable times to perform life liberations include the time when someone encounters their predestined calamities, such as prior to hospitalisation or a major operation, after being diagnosed with severe illness, or after being involved in unfortunate incidents such as a car accident, etc. To achieve the best results, it is best to choose a sunny day when Yang energy is at its peak. Avoid doing it at night time; cloudy or rainy days are fine during the daytime.

4. It is best to release animals that are commonly consumed by humans, including fish, shrimp, prawns, crabs, clams, etc. Other animals that tend to be killed or eaten would also be suitable.

5. You should recite sutras and mantras when you perform life liberations. Performing life liberations helps us to eliminate disasters and extend our lifespans; reciting mantras and sutras helps to protect us. For best results, it is suggested that you perform both together. You can start reciting on your way to the releasing site. It is best to recite the **Great Compassionate Mantra**. Before you recite, you

should state your full name: "May the Greatly Merciful and Greatly Compassionate Guan Yin Bodhisattva protect and bless me, <your full name>, help me to eliminate disasters and extend my lifespan. I will continue accumulating more merits and virtues." Then you can recite the *Great Compassion Mantra*, the more times the better. If you are performing life liberation on behalf of someone else, you can say, "May the Greatly Merciful and Greatly Compassionate Guan Yin Bodhisattva protect and bless <full name>, help him/her to eliminate disasters and extend his/her lifespan."

6. Once you arrive at the releasing site, you can face the sky and say the following prayer three times, "I express my sincere gratitude to the Greatly Merciful and Greatly Compassionate Guan Yin Bodhisattva". Then you can recite the *Great Compassion Mantra* and *Heart Sutra* once each, and the *Qi Fo Mie Zui Zhen Yan* 7 times. Just before you release the fish into the water, you can say the prayer once more, "<Full name> is releasing <number or total weight> of <fish, shrimp, or other creatures being released>. May the Greatly Merciful and Greatly Compassionate Guan Yin Bodhisattva protect and bless <full name>, help <full name> to eliminate disasters and extend the lifespan of <full name>." While you are releasing fish, you can also recite the *Great Compassion Mantra*, the *Heart Sutra*, and the *Amitabha Pure Land Rebirth Mantra* as many times as you like. The more the better. Be gentle when you release the fish into the water so that it will not cause them any harm.

7. If any of the creatures to be released die during life liberation, you need to recite the **Amitabha Pure Land Rebirth Mantra** to help the spirits of the deceased ascend to a higher spiritual realm. Generally, you need to recite 3 times for each shrimp or prawn, 7 times for each crab and 7 times for each fish that died.

8. It is best to use your own money to purchase the creatures to be released. If you are releasing on behalf of your family members, it is best to use their money to make the purchase. When you use your own money to perform a life liberation on behalf of others, you can say the following prayer to Guan Yin Bodhisattva beforehand, "May the Greatly Merciful and Greatly Compassionate Guan Yin Bodhisattva forgive me, <your full name>, I am now using my money to perform life liberation for <full name of the family member or friend>." After this, you can purchase fish and perform the life liberation, which will be effective then. Alternatively, before you perform life liberation, you can say the following prayer at your altar: "I, <your full name>, will give <amount of money> to <full name of the family member or friend>. Please regard this money as his/hers."

9. If your family members or friends do not believe in life liberation, or even object to your doing it, then the effects of performing life liberation on their behalf will be reduced. However, performing life liberation for them would be better than not performing it at all.

10. Once you arrive at the site of life liberation, it is best not to mention your name again. If you frequently state your name, or think about your name in your mind, a portion of the merits and virtues from performing the life liberation would be allocated to you. Simply say the following, "<full name of the family member or friend> has purchased <quantity or weight of fish>. May the Greatly Merciful and Greatly Compassionate Guan Yin Bodhisattva protect and bless <full name of the family member or friend>". Alternatively, you can write the name of the person and the quantity or weight of fish on a piece of paper and read it out at the site.

11. After you have performed life liberation on behalf of others, it would be best if you let them know the amount of fish that you have released for them. However, if they are completely against the practice of performing life liberation, it would be best not to mention anything to them at all. This is to prevent them from creating karma of speech.

4. Making Great Vows

Performing recitations, making vows, and performing life liberations are the Three Golden Buddhist Practices given by the Greatly Merciful and Greatly Compassionate Guan Yin Bodhisattva. We must learn to use them well. Among these, the power of vows is very important to every Buddhist practitioner. Making vows involves saying your prayer quietly or softly in front of Guan Yin Bodhisattva, praying to the Bodhisattva for protection, blessings, or to perform miracles, to resolve your problems, confusions, disasters, misfortunes, etc. As part of the prayer, you will vow to do one or more of the following things:

- Adopt a vegetarian diet on the 1st and 15th day of every lunar month for the rest of your life;
- Not eat freshly killed seafood or other creatures for the rest of your life;
- Not perform the act of killing (including animals) for the rest of your life;
- Persistently perform good deeds every day;
- Offer gold plating for statues of Buddhas and Bodhisattvas;
- Introduce Buddhism to <number of> people within <a certain period of time>, helping them awaken and be free from suffering;
- Accumulate merits and virtues by performing meritorious and virtuous deeds, such as making donations to print

<number of> Buddhist scriptures or books;

- Distribute or donate <number of> books and CDs to sentient beings.

1. If you have made a vow to go vegetarian on every 1st and 15th of the lunar month, but later you have forgotten about it or you are unable to fulfil the vow due to special circumstances, you can inform Guan Yin Bodhisattva in advance, and practise vegetarianism on an earlier or later date. Alternatively, you can make a vow to adopt a vegetarian diet for two days every month instead of specifying on the 1st and 15th of each lunar month. This allows more flexibility.

2. Once you have made a vow, you must consistently keep your vow. If you cannot keep your vow simply due to personal reasons, then you will certainly receive punishment.

3. After you have your prayers answered by Bodhisattvas, you should return to the same temple where you originally made the vows to fulfil them before the statues of Buddhas and Bodhisattvas. You can fulfil your vows by making incense offerings, making prostrations, donations and performing meritorious and virtuous deeds. The amount of donations that you make and the amount of merits you contribute do not matter, as long as it is within your ability and you are sincerely expressing your gratitude. If you have made the great vows to go vegetarian and to

introduce Buddhism to people, etc., then you should persevere in your practice. This is also a form of fulfilling your vows.

5. Setting Up
Altars and Making Offerings

If conditions allow, it is best to have an altar at home for you to pay respects and make offerings to Buddhas and Bodhisattvas. You should also invite a statue of Guan Yin Bodhisattva to your altar.

1. The basic requirements for altar setup at home are as follows:

- The altar must not be near a toilet (the toilet door should be closed at all times).

- The altar must not directly face the kitchen.

- The altar must not be placed on top of the television, refrigerator, or directly below an air conditioner. If it is close to the television or in an untidy environment, you can use a cabinet with a wooden door for the altar. When you are not offering incense, you can close the door. When you are offering incense, please do not switch on the television. You should also not cover the statues or images of Buddhas or Bodhisattvas with a glass dome.

- You should not place the altar in the bedroom of a couple (the bedroom of an elderly couple may be alright).

- You can place the altar in single bedrooms, but the foot of the bed should not face the altar.

- You should not place the altar on a balcony extending out from the building (i.e. not attached to the ground). However, if the balcony is inside the building then it would be alright, e.g. sunroom.

- All statues and images of Buddhas and Bodhisattvas, as well as other Dharma instruments, including incense burners, oil lamps, etc. should not be placed on an extended fixture (jutting out over empty space). In other words, there must be tables, cabinets or frames, etc. that are connected to the ground to hold up the items.
  - o The best location to make offerings and pray to Buddhas and Bodhisattvas is near a window where it is bright. But you should not place the altar against a window; the altar must be placed against a wall. There should not be any mirrors in its surroundings.
  - o Do not place unrelated objects or books underneath the altar. Normally, Buddhist scriptures and Dharma instruments could be stored underneath.
  - o The altar should not be too high or too low. It would be best if the statues or images of Buddhas and Bodhisattvas on your altar are slightly above eye level. If they are too low, you can place something (such as a nice box) underneath to raise their height.
  - o On the altar, there should be oil lamps (offering oil lamps can improve your eye health), and cups of water (one cup of water for each statue or image of Buddhas and Bodhisattvas). The water should be

changed daily. Do not drink the water directly from the cup used for offerings.

o   There should be a burner for the offering of incense. You can make an incense offering once in the morning and once at night. The time for incense offerings should be kept consistent. The best times for the morning offerings are 6am, 8am and 10am, and the best times for night offerings are 6pm, 8pm and 10pm.

o   It is best not to have too many statues or images of Buddhas and Bodhisattvas on the altar.

o   If conditions allow, you can make offerings of fresh fruit (allowing wishes to come true more quickly) and fresh flowers (offering fresh flowers can improve your physical attractiveness). Fruits and flowers should not be left on the altar longer than one week. If they are not fresh, remove or replace them as soon as possible. Do not leave rotten fruits and withered flowers on the altar even if replacements are not available.

o   The best location for the altar is sitting south and facing north (for the Southern Hemisphere), or sitting north and facing south (for the Northern Hemisphere). However, if your current conditions do not allow you to place the altar this way, other directions are also acceptable.

2. Offering Fruit:

- It is best to offer fruits that are fragrant, such as apples, oranges, mangoes, pineapples, watermelons, etc.

- Bananas and peaches are not suitable for offering to Buddhas and Bodhisattvas.

- The fruits offered should be in odd number for each layer, not the total number.

- For example, if four fruits are offered, they should be arranged in such a way that there are three at the bottom layer with one on top. In short, every layer should be in odd number.

- Offer only one type of fruit on each plate. Do not offer an assortment of fruits on one plate.

- The total number of plates of fruits does not matter.

- When replacing fruits, replace the whole plate of fruits. Do not remove a few from the plate and add fresh ones to the old ones.

3. Offering Flowers:

- It is good to offer lucky bamboo to Buddhas and Bodhisattvas.

- Chrysanthemums, lilies, orchids, and daffodils can be offered to Buddhas and Bodhisattvas. Roses are not suitable for offering due to their thorns.

- You can tell whether a flower is suitable for offerings or not by its Chinese name. For example, flowers such as peach blossoms or Japanese morning glories are not suitable offerings.

- Potted plants with soil must not be placed on the altar.

- In general, when offering lucky bamboo, place one vase on each side of the altar. It is alright to offer one, two or three lucky bamboos in each vase, but not too many.

4. Offering Oil:

- If possible, the number of oil lamps should match the number of statues/images of Buddhas and Bodhisattvas on the altar. If this is not possible, you may offer a pair of oil lamps or a single oil lamp for the entire altar.

- If you have one statue/image of Bodhisattva on the altar, you can offer one oil lamp. Offering two oil lamps is fine as well.

- Practitioners following Guan Yin Citta Dharma Door usually pray to these six Bodhisattvas: Guan Yin Bodhisattva, Nanjing Bodhisattva, Tai Sui Bodhisattva, Guan Di Bodhisattva, Zhou Tsang Bodhisattva and Guan Ping Bodhisattva. It is best to have 4 oil lamps (one for Guan Yin Bodhisattva, one for Nanjing Bodhisattva, one for Tai Sui Bodhisattva, and a shared one for Guan Di Bodhisattva, Zhou Tsang Bodhisattva and Guan Ping Bodhisattva. If possible, it would be best to have 6 oil lamps (Offer separate oil lamps for Zhou Tsang Bodhisattva and Guan Ping Bodhisattva). If this is not possible, then you should only put one or two oil lamps for the entire altar.

- The offering of candles is generally not recommended. If you have been doing so, it is best to offer a pair of red candles.

- You are advised to put out the oil lamps as soon as you are done with your prayer or before the incense is burnt out. Avoid leaving oil lamps burning while there is no burning incense, as this tends to attract foreign spirits.

- You may use electric lotus lamps provided that you are offering real oil lamps at the same time. Take note that they must not be switched on all day long (24 hours).

- To make incense offerings and perform prostration, you can first turn on the electric lotus lamps and then light the oil lamps. Before the incense is burnt out, you need to put out the oil lamps, and then switch off the electric lotus lamps.

- You can put out the oil lamps by covering the flame with a lid or with other suitable instruments. Do not blow them out with your mouth.

- Leaving lotus lamps on for a long period of time without offering incense tends to attract foreign spirits.

- Making offerings of vegetable oil to Buddhas and Bodhisattvas will result in blessings of keen eyesight, hearing and wisdom.

- Generally, vegetable oils such as olive oil, canola seed oil, corn oil, and lotus oil may be used in oil offerings.

- Sesame oil, peanut oil, or any oil with an aroma should not be used for oil lamps, as oils with an aroma are considered impure. Their strong aroma would overpower the scent of the sandalwood incense, thus they are not suitable for offerings to Buddhas and Bodhisattvas.

- Soybean oil is too concentrated to burn easily, and is therefore also unsuitable for oil offerings.

- After removing the packaging and the label, you can offer the entire bottle of oil before the Buddhas and Bodhisattvas on the altar. This would be considered an oil offering, too.

- However, the best way of making oil offerings is to light oil lamps and refill the oil lamps with the oil that you wish to offer. You should refill the oil lamps frequently by adding a little bit of fresh oil every day, just as you would make offerings of fresh flowers, fruit and water.

- Be aware that the oil that has been offered to Buddhas and Bodhisattvas must not be used to cook non-vegetarian dishes. We can consume the fruits and water after offering them to Buddhas and Bodhisattvas directly. But for the offered oil, it has to be cooked before being consumed. For example, you may use the offered oil to cook vegetarian dishes.

- When you make oil offerings in a public place, for example, at the Guan Yin Practice Centre, you can bring your own bottle of oil to refill the oil lamps on the altar. Afterwards, you can take the bottle home and use the remaining oil for cooking purposes.

5. Great Compassion Water:

• Great Compassion Water is the water that you have offered to Guan Yin Bodhisattva. It has been blessed by Guan Yin Bodhisattva. As ordinary humans, we are unable to bless the water simply by performing recitations to make it become Great Compassion Water.

• You can offer hot or cold water that has previously been boiled, mineral water, purified water or any other potable water that has no colour or fragrance. You should not directly use tap water or untreated water.

• Please use a brand new cup for making water offerings for Great Compassion Water. The cup can be made of glass, china or ceramic. It can be with or without a lid, but it is better to have a lid to prevent dust and insects from falling into the cup. It is best to use a plain white cup without any text on it. There should not be any scriptures including the **Great Compassion Mantra** or the **Heart Sutra** printed on the cup. The cup should also not have any names or images of Buddhas or Bodhisattvas, or have any animal figures.

• Generally, one cup of water is offered to each Buddha or Bodhisattva. You could offer more than one cup of water before each Buddha or Bodhisattva, but you should not have fewer cups than the number of Buddhas or Bodhisattvas on the altar. The cup should not be too large in size. In addition, you should not offer bottled mineral water to Buddhas and Bodhisattvas, it is disrespectful to substitute the cup of water with a bottle of mineral water. While you are offering cups of water, bottled water should not be offered on the altar.

- You should not drink the Great Compassion Water directly from the cup used for offering on the altar. The water can be poured from the offering cup to another cup for drinking. Your mouth should not touch the offering cup. As a general practice, you can first face the statues and images of Buddhas and Bodhisattvas, then with both hands, respectfully raise the cup slightly above your eyebrows, and say the following prayer gently: "May the Greatly Merciful and Greatly Compassionate Guan Yin Bodhisattva protect and bless me, <your full name>, grant me good health." At the same time, you can visualise that the pure water of Guan Yin Bodhisattva is gradually being poured onto the top of your head, and then flowing over your entire body. You can then pour the water into another cup, and drink the water respectfully. For best results, you can place your palm facing down over the cup and recite the **Great Compassion Mantra** once before drinking the water.

- After the water has been offered, if you find the water too cold and you wish to heat it up, avoid doing so directly or using the microwave. You can immerse the container with the Great Compassion Water in hot water to heat it up before drinking (it should only be heated slightly rather than heated to its boiling point).

- For the water offered to other Buddhas and Bodhisattvas, you can just pour it away. Otherwise, you need to recite the **Great Compassion Mantra** once before drinking. In addition, you should not mix the water that you offered to different Buddhas and Bodhisattvas together. You should pour the water into different cups before drinking.

- Water offered to Buddhas and Bodhisattvas should not be used for watering plants.

6. Incense Burners and Offering of Incense and Grand Incense

- For the altar in the home, incense should be offered at least twice a day, once in the morning and once at night. The time of incense offerings should be kept consistent. The best times for the morning offerings are 6am, 8pm and 10am and for night offerings, 6pm, 8pm, and 10pm. Incense offering is optional if recitations of scriptures and *Little Houses* are being performed at other times. If conditions permit, it is good to keep the incense burning.

- If you have several statues or images of Bodhisattvas on the altar, it is best to place one incense burner before each statue. You can offer one incense stick for each incense burner and three incense sticks on the first and fifteenth day of each lunar month as well as commemorative days of Buddhas and Bodhisattvas. If conditions do not allow, you can place only one incense burner for the entire altar but it is best to light three incense sticks for the morning and night offerings of incense.

- You may offer grand incense on the 1st and 15th day of each lunar month and commemorative days of Buddhas and Bodhisattvas. After lighting the oil lamps and making incense offerings, you can then light a piece of sandalwood (available in most Buddhist shops). Extinguish the flame by fanning it with your hand; the smoke that comes out is considered grand incense, the fragrance of Buddhas and Bodhisattvas. You must not blow it out with your mouth. You can repeat this offering three times, after which you can make prostrations, say your prayers and perform recitations of scriptures. The used sandalwood can be placed horizontally in the incense burner and be kept for future use.

7. Setting Up Altar When Moving House:

- If you already have an altar in your existing home, you need to invite the statue of Bodhisattva to your new home. First, burn the last stick of incense in your old home, wait for the incense to burn out, then invite the statue down from the altar and wrap it with a piece of red cloth. When you arrive at your new home, it is important that you place the statue of Bodhisattva on the altar first, and then make incense offerings with three incense sticks. Recite the **Great Compassion Mantra** 7 times and the **Heart Sutra** 7 times, make more prostrations, and say the following prayer: "May the Greatly Merciful and Greatly Compassionate Guan Yin Bodhisattva come to our new home, please continue to protect and bless me, <full name>, and my family (full names of family members). We will cultivate our minds diligently and sincerely." It is best to relocate your altar and set it up before you move the rest of your belongings.

- When you relocate your altar to your new home, it is not necessary to perform another blessing ceremony for the statue of Bodhisattva. This is because the Bodhisattva has already visited the statue. The Bodhisattva will visit your home once an incense offering is made.

- If the house is under renovation and you have to stay at another place temporarily, it is best that you set up an altar at the temporary residence. When the new home is ready, you can move the altar there.

8. Making Offerings When Away Temporarily:

- If you have to be away for a brief period (e.g. business trip etc.), you can replace the Great Compassion Water, fruit and flowers shortly before leaving. Make sure they won't rot before your return. Leave everything as they are on the altar; it is not necessary to cover them.

- It is best to take a photo of the altar when there is no incense burning. Wrap the photo with a piece of red cloth and bring it with you. If conditions permit, you can make offerings of incense, water, fruit, and flowers in front of the photo. If conditions do not allow, just take the photo out and offer Heart Incense, and then wrap the photo with the red cloth after finishing.

9. Inviting Bodhisattva to Enter the Sacred Image:

- If you are following Master Lu's Guan Yin Citta Dharma Door to cultivate your mind and practise Buddhism, it is best to invite a statue or an image of Guan Yin Bodhisattva to the altar in your home. At the same time, we must respect all religions, all Buddhas and Bodhisattvas, and all spiritual beings. In terms of the statue or image of Guan Yin Bodhisattva we invite, generally it is better to choose one in a standing posture holding the purification vase and the willow branch, made of ceramic, and which contains no dragon or other auspicious creatures. It is also recommended that you select a new statue or image that has not been blessed. You can bring the statue or image home and perform the blessing ceremony on your own to invite Bodhisattva to enter the statue. It is certainly better to have Master Lu or other esteemed, knowledgeable and greatly virtuous Buddhist monastic or lay practitioners bless the statue or image for you.

- When you select a statue or image of Guan Yin Bodhisattva, you can go to a Buddhist shop and look at the ones that you wish to invite home. If you feel that you favour a particular statue or image, or if you feel that the statue or image of Bodhisattva is smiling at you, then you should invite that statue or image home. You can also invite the image of Guan Yin Bodhisattva from the Guan Yin Centre after you colour print and frame it.

- Generally, if you have not attained a great spiritual state, you do not have the ability to bless statues or images of Buddhas and Bodhisattvas yourself. However, you can still invite Guan Yin Bodhisattva to enter a statue or image on your altar. On an auspicious day such as the 1st or 15th day of the lunar month, and during an auspicious time such as 6am or 8am (or 4pm if it is not possible in the morning), you can prepare the altar where the statue or image is going to be placed. After you have invited the statue or image of Guan Yin Bodhisattva to your altar, you can make offerings of water, fruit, oil, and incense. It is better to make incense offerings with three incense sticks. Join your palms together and raise the incense sticks slightly above your head, and bow to Guan Yin Bodhisattva 3 times. After you place the incense sticks into the incense burner in front of the statue or image of Guan Yin Bodhisattva, you can say the following prayer: "May the Greatly Merciful and Greatly Compassionate Guan Yin Bodhisattva perform miracles, and enter the sacred <statue or image> offered by me, <your full name>". You should then recite the **Great Compassion Mantra** 7 times and **Heart Sutra** 7 times, and then prostrate 3 more times. The more you recite the **Great Compassion Mantra** and the **Heart Sutra**, the better the result.

- Before you begin your recitation, you can say your prayers to Guan Yin Bodhisattva. For example, you can sincerely pray to Guan Yin Bodhisattva for protection and blessings, and to grant your family safety and harmony. You can also make a vow that from now on you will pay respect to Guan Yin Bodhisattva twice a day, once in the morning and once at night, etc. Ensure that your incense sticks are burning during the entire recitation process.

- After you have invited the statues or images of Buddhas and Bodhisattvas to your altar, avoid touching the statues or images randomly. In general, you do not need to clean the statues or images frequently. If too much dust has accumulated, you may clean it gently with a new piece of dry cloth during the daytime and recite the *Heart Sutra* while cleaning. Should you ever need to relocate the statues or images, you should first make an incense offering to the Buddhas and Bodhisattvas, and tell Bodhisattvas about the relocation. Then you should recite the *Great Compassion Mantra* 3 times, and the *Heart Sutra* 3 times. After the incense has completely finished burning, you can then relocate the statues or images (during the daytime) while reciting the *Heart Sutra*.

10. Offering Heart Incense

- If you are unable to set up an altar in your home for the time being, or you are away on a business trip or vacation, you can offer the Heart Incense.

- Method: When offering the Heart Incense, visualise that the image of Guan Yin Bodhisattva is in front of you. Visualise that you are making an oil lamp offering, followed by taking an incense stick and lighting the incense, joining your palms together and then raising the incense above your forehead between your eyebrows. Then you visualise that you are placing the incense into the incense burner, making full prostrations, and saying your prayers in your heart. Do not do any other actions such as bowing or physically kneeling down.

- Please note: You can only make incense offerings if you have an altar at home where you pay respects and make offerings to Buddhas and Bodhisattvas every day. Images of Buddhas and Bodhisattvas on computer screens, printed on sutra booklets or other statues and images of Buddhas and Bodhisattvas that you do not pay respects and make offerings to every day would not have the energy field of Buddhas and Bodhisattvas. If you are making incense offerings to these statues or images, then you are actually making offerings to heaven and earth, and all the spiritual beings around you might come and accept your offerings. This involves risks and may invite unnecessary troubles.

11. Setting up an altar in the home under constraints

- Due to the constraints in your living place, for example, if it is impossible to avoid the bedroom of a couple, kitchen or toilet, or there are family members who do not believe in Buddhism at the moment, you may buy a new cabinet with a wooden door in which to place the statue of Guan Yin Bodhisattva.

- Other than praying instruments and Buddhist sutra booklets, do not place any unrelated items in the cabinet or anywhere above the statue.

- You may keep the cabinet door open while offering incense to the Bodhisattva. Close the cabinet door once the incense has finished burning.

12. Procedures to set up an altar in the home

(1). Prepare the following items and respectfully place them on the altar.

a. Statues/images of Buddhas and Bodhisattvas (Arrange them in the following order when you stand facing the altar. The number is the order for you to place the statues/images on the altar); ③Tai Sui Bodhisattva; ②Nanjing Bodhisattva; ① Guan Yin Bodhisattva; ④Guan Di Bodhisattva (Guan Ping Bodhisattva, Guan Di Bodhisattva, Zhou Tsang Bodhisattva).

b. Incense burner;

c. Oil lamp;

d. Cups of water;

e. Fruit;

f. Flowers.

(2). Inviting Bodhisattvas

- Light up the oil lamps. If you have electric lotus lamps, switch them on first before lighting oil lamps.

- Light up incense sticks. Light up 3 incense sticks from the oil lamp. Raise the incense sticks slightly above your forehead between your eyebrows and bow 3 times. Place the 3 incenses all at once into the incense burner, do not separate them and do not point the incense sticks to Buddhas and Bodhisattvas.

- Light up grand incense (sandalwood) 3 times. First light up the oil lamp and incense sticks, then burn the sandalwood using the oil lamp. Put out the flame on the sandalwood (do not blow with your mouth) and the smoke that comes out is considered grand incense, the fragrance of Bodhisattvas. This can be repeated three times.

- Kneel down in front of the Bodhisattvas

- Sincerely invite the Bodhisattvas (Mention the holy names of each Bodhisattva three times)

- You may say this prayer, "May the Greatly Merciful and Greatly Compassion Guan Yin Bodhisattva perform miracles, and enter the sacred (statue or image) offered by me, (your full name)." You should then recite the *Great Compassion Mantra* 7 times and the *Heart Sutra* 7 times. Likewise, you request Guan Yin Bodhisattva to invite Nanjing Bodhisattva to enter sacred statue/image offered by you, after which you recite the holy name of Nanjing Bodhisattva 108 times. Next, you request Guan Yin Bodhisattva to invite Tai Sui Bodhisattva to enter the sacred image offered by you, then you recite the holy name of Tai Sui Bodhisattva 108 times, followed by *Xiao Zai Ji Xiang Shen Zhou* 21 times. Similarly, you request Guan Yin Bodhisattva to invite Guan Di Bodhisattva, Zhou Tsang Bodhisattva and Guan Ping Bodhisattva to enter the sacred statues/images offered by you, and then recite their holy names 108 times.

- If the statues or images have been blessed by Master Lu,

you can pray to them straight away and need not make separate recitations. You can make a general invitation for the Bodhisattvas to enter the sacred statues of images offered by you, after which you recite the **Great Compassion Mantra** 7 times and the **Heart Sutra** 7 times.

- Kneel down and bow once to each Bodhisattva. Alternatively, you can pay general respects to all the Bodhisattvas by bowing 7 times.

- Subsequently, you may make a wish and say your prayer according to your conditions:

  (1). Making vows: Not to kill live creatures for the rest of your life; practise vegetarianism; make incense offerings once in the morning and once at night, introduce Buddhism to others and help them awaken spiritually; perform meritorious and virtuous deeds by making donations to print sutra booklets and CDs for free distribution. You should make vows according to your ability and circumstances. It is inappropriate to demand that everyone make specific vows.

  (2). Saying prayers: Make reasonable wishes based on your own circumstances. For example, you may pray for good health, success in your career and harmony in the family.

- Express your gratitude:
  Finally express your gratitude to the Bodhisattvas by bowing 7 times.
  "My sincere gratitude to Namo the Greatly Merciful and Greatly Compassionate Guan Yin Bodhisattva Mo He Sa".

"My sincere gratitude to Namo Nanjing Bodhisattva, Namo Tai Sui Bodhisattva, Namo Guan Di Bodhisattva, Namo Zhou Tsang Bodhisattva, Namo Guan Ping Bodhisattva", and include each Bodhisattva you make offerings to on the altar, if any.

"My sincere gratitude to all Buddhas and Bodhisattvas, and Dharma Protectors".

6. Application for Change of Name

Your name represents your spirit. When your name is called, your souls and spirits follow your name.

When a person is born, the name written on the birth certificate is also recorded in the spiritual realms: heaven and the underworld. If you have changed your name and used your new name for years, it is likely that your new name has become active spiritually. In this situation you can use your new name to perform daily recitations and address your *Little Houses*. However, it is still advisable to lodge the *Application for Change of Name* (A sample can be found in **Appendix B**).

When you lodge the *Application for Change of Name*, you are also updating your new name with Buddhas, Bodhisattvas, officers who are in charge of name changes in the heaven and the underworld, and all other spiritual beings.

You can download the *Application for Change of Name* form at www.GuanYinCitta.com.

Use yellow A4 size paper to print the application form. Fill in both your original name and new name on the application form. Fill in your original name where it says, "Devotee's original full name", and your new name where it says, "Now changed to" and "Devotee's full name". If you are lodging the *Application for Change of Name* on behalf of your child or family members, please fill in the applicant's date of birth according to the Gregorian calendar.

Fill in your current location, which is the location where you are going to perform the ritual to lodge *the Application for Change of Name*, in the "Location" field (e.g. "Beijing, China" or "Sydney, Australia"). Finally, fill in the date field, using the date of burning the application form.

It is best to burn the application form on a sunny day. The best times are 6am, 8am and 4pm.

Instead of printing, you can also hand-write the form on a yellow piece of A4 sized paper based on the *Application for Change of Name* form at www.GuanYinCitta.com.

You can lodge the application form at home if you have a Buddhist altar. First, light the oil lamp(s), then offer incense and read out the application in front of your altar (you may kneel while reading it). Then recite the **Great Compassion Mantra** 7 times and the **Heart Sutra** 7 times before burning the application form (from top to bottom).

If you do not have a Buddhist altar at home, then you can go to a Buddhist temple to lodge your application. You should first kneel and bow to every Buddha and Bodhisattva at the temple, then read out your application in the Guan Yin Hall, in front of Guan Yin Bodhisattva, "I, <your full name>, come to <name of the temple> today, to pay my respect to all Buddhas and Bodhisattvas in this temple. May the Greatly Merciful and Greatly Compassionate Guan Yin Bodhisattva be my witness and verify that my original name <old name> has been changed to <new name>. May all the Buddhas and Bodhisattvas in this temple be my witnesses." Next recite the

Great Compassion Mantra 7 times and the *Heart Sutra* 7 times before burning your application form (from top to bottom) in the container where incense sticks or papers are burnt.

You only need to lodge your application once. If, for some reason, you think that your *Application for Change of Name* did not go through you can lodge your application again.

It is best if you can lodge the *Application for Change of Name* personally. If a child is too young and is unable to perform the ritual, parents or other family members can lodge the application on behalf of the child.

You do not need to lodge the application for a deceased person. Just use the name they used most often while they were alive.

If you have been called by several names in the past and now you want to lodge the *Application for Change of Name*, you can pick the name that has been used most often as your original name (generally names that have been used for more than a decade are already active spiritually). Alternatively, you can also write all the names that have been used in the past under "Devotee's original full name."

If you are unsure of your original name, for example, if you were adopted, you can lodge the *Application for True Name*. You can download the *Application for True Name* form from www.GuanYinCitta.com (A sample can be found in **Appendix C**).

How to determine whether the *Application for Change of Name* has been successfully lodged?

1. Your instincts play an important role. First of all, it is mostly based on the feelings of the person who changes their name. Generally, we change our names to improve our conditions. After having lodged the *Application for Change of Name,* you should feel happier, as if you have opened up your heart and eased your mind. You should sense an immediate improvement in your mood and that your fortunes are already changing for the better. If you experience the above, your application is successful. If, after lodging the application, you feel the same or even worse than before, or have bad feelings, then your application may not have been successful, or your new name may not be suitable for you.

2. Second, you should recite more of the **Heart Sutra**. People who do more recitations of the **Heart Sutra** will grow in wisdom, and form a connection with their new names. When others call you by your new name, or during special occasions when your name is used, you will know that the new name is associated with you.

3. Third, the success of lodging the application is also determined by the energy field of the new name. Has your new name been used by someone else? If someone else is already using that name, and your energy field is very close to this person, it would be very difficult for your new name to take effect.

4. Fourth, it is essential for the *Application for Change of Name* to be active spiritually. For example, if you changed your name over ten years ago without lodging the *Application for Change of Name,* then this name should be active spiritually to some extent since you have been called by this name for over ten years. However, as you have never lodged the *Application for Change of Name,* this name has not been officially registered in the spirit world, your spirits and soul tend to depart from the body very easily. Therefore, once you have lodged the *Application for Change of Name,* you should be called by your new name in full as many times as possible. It usually takes three months to 100 days for the new name to be active spiritually.

5. Fifth, you can recite *Little Houses* addressed to the "Karmic Creditors of <your new full name>" and observe the effects after burning them. For example, if you used to feel lethargic and have nightmares but now you can see improvement in your condition, then it indicates that your *Application for Change of Name* has been successful.

Once you have lodged your application, each day before reciting sutras and mantras you can say your new name a few more times to Buddhas and Bodhisattvas in front of the altar. This is very helpful in allowing your new name to take effect.

Before lodging your application, you can begin by reading out the text on the application form once. Then you can recite the **Great Compassion Mantra** 7 times and the **Heart Sutra** 7 times. As the final step, you can burn the application form.

It is better to lodge the application on the 1st and 15th day of the lunar month, as these days are auspicious and favourable. The best times to lodge the application are 6am and 8am.

If your application is unsuccessful, you can lodge it multiple times until it is successful.

Generally, as soon as you have lodged your application, you can start using your new name to fill out your *Little House*. If you are unsure whether your application is successful for the time being, you can address your *Little House* to the "Karmic Creditor of <your new name> (<your old name>)". This format can only be used temporarily as an interim solution and should not be used in the long term.

If your application is unsuccessful after your first attempt, but you have recited and burnt your *Little Houses* using your new name, these *Little Houses* will still be effective as soon as your application is successful in your later attempt.

7. Application for
Convincing Family Members

It requires great blessings to have both partners in a marriage or even the entire family to perform recitations and practise Buddhism together. If you have already started practicing Buddhism, you can gradually introduce it to your family members. You can show your family members some of Master Lu's books and ask them to listen to the radio programs if they understand Chinese. You could tell them "These books and programs are really interesting, let's study them together". If your family members are not interested, do not force them. It is best to act in accordance with karmic conditions, not cling to them.

You can recite the *Heart Sutra* 7 times per day for each of your family members. Before you begin your recitation, you can say the following prayer "May the Greatly Merciful and Greatly Compassionate Guan Yin Bodhisattva protect and bless <your family member's name>, help <family member> to gain wisdom, believe in Buddhism and start performing recitations." You can continue doing this for as long as necessary.

When you recite the *Heart Sutra* for your family members, it is best not to tell them so as to prevent them from feeling uncomfortable or offended, which can easily lead them to create the karma of speech. If your family members still do not believe in Buddhism after more than a month of reciting the *Heart Sutra* (7 times per day) for them, you can lodge an application to Guan Yin Bodhisattva and state your prayer.

1. Download the *Application for Convincing Family Members* from www.GuanYinCitta.com (A sample can be found in *Appendix D*). Print the application form on a yellow A4 piece of paper (**Caution: Do not burn this application form**).

2. Use a black or blue pen to write the full name and date of birth of your family member (according to the Gregorian calendar), and your full name.

3. Every day during the daytime (the best times are 6am, 8am, 4pm and 10pm, but it is best to avoid night time), light oil lamps and make incense offerings at your home altar.

4. Read out the text on the application form once, and then place the application form on the altar. If your altar is small, you can place the application form underneath the incense burner.

5. Kneel and make a full bow (with your forehead touching the floor) to Buddhas and Bodhisattvas.

6. Recite the *Heart Sutra*, generally 7 times or more.

7. Once you have completed your recitations or the incense has finished burning, it is best to fold the *Application for Convincing Family Members* and put it away. The *Application for Convincing Family Members* must not be left on the altar for a long period of time, as this may cause the relevant family member to have fits of temper

and their soul to depart from their body or be incomplete.

8. The above procedure for lodging the *Application for Convincing Family Members* can be performed once a day.

This is a very serious Buddhist ritual and it is best performed after you have recited the **Heart Sutra** 7 times per day for your family members over a long period of time (usually longer than one month). It is best to perform this without informing the relevant family members so as to prevent them from feeling uncomfortable or offended, which can easily lead them to create the karma of speech.

Once the application has been successful, the application form can be put aside for 1 to 2 months. After this time, you can place the application form in an envelope and then dispose of it. **Caution: Do not burn the application form.**

8. Personal Experiences and Inspirational Stories

Due to limited space, here we can only include a portion of the shared personal experiences of practising Guan Yin Citta Dharma Door. For more personal testimonies, please visit our official website: www.GuanYinCitta.com

1. Venerable Shi Xin Wu's Account

I express my deep gratitude to Bodhisattvas,

My deep gratitude to Guan Yin Bodhisattva,

My deep gratitude to all Bodhisattvas,

My deep gratitude to Master Jun Hong Lu,

Gratitude to Great Senior Monks and Nuns,

Thank you to all Monks and Nuns,

Thank you to the Malaysian Team,

And thank you to all disciples and participants. You are so great.

I am French and from Paris. I used to be a professor and a teacher with several very famous educational institutions. I'm now 53 years old.

I have been following Master Lu to practise Guan Yin Citta Dharma Door for five years. And I have also been a vegetarian for five years.

On 24 December 2016, I became a disciple of Master Lu's, here in Kuala Lumpur. On that day I had special and overwhelming feelings! A marvellous feeling, a wonderful feeling, a feeling of great peace.

When Master Lu put his hand on my head, I felt like I was reborn again, like a father taking you in his arms, saying "Son, I'm proud of you".

A heart-warming feeling naturally arose within me and it made me cry from joy and peace.

Don't hesitate to become a disciple!

May I tell you how I feel for the first time in my life? Do you want to hear?

I am very happy!

Firstly, because I'm here with you!

Secondly, because like you, I'm here to listen to Master Lu's Dharma Talk!

Thirdly, because I'm in Malaysia, a wonderful country where people are so nice. I have great Buddhist friends here who have helped me to practise Buddhism, and my life has been totally changed.

Why is this Buddhist a foreigner, a white person and following Guan Yin Bodhisattva and Master Lu?

I can see this question in your eyes.

No problem. I can give you the answer now.

It's simple. The reason is that they are very kind to us and take care of us.

Our world is special. There are a lot of stress, problems, difficulties, and risks:

Health, human relations, money, transportation, kids' education, time, work, and societal pressures such as beauty, trends, fashion and so on...

Have a look! More and more pollution, global warming, animals and plants are disappearing!

Why did I stop working, stop earning money, and choose to become a Buddhist and a vegetarian, and trust Guan Yin Bodhisattva and Master Lu?

Because they show us the right path to happiness, guide us to achieve joy and live a healthy and blissful life, and help us go to Heaven.

I can list a hundred examples of the benefits of practising Guan Yin Citta Dharma Door.

Before, I had a lot of health issues, like heart problems, and I nearly died. I had high blood pressure and suffered from headaches all the time as well as other health problems.

This is finished. I have a good health now because I'm a vegetarian. I recite Buddhist scriptures and *Little Houses*, release fish, and follow Master Lu's teachings.

I wasted a lot of time of my life. I have done a lot of things that left me empty handed.

Although I was happy, it was just a feeling and an illusion, not real happiness. My health was deteriorating.

I prayed to Guan Yin Bodhisattva for help many times and, of course, I followed what Master Lu taught us: Release fish, recite Buddhist scriptures and *Little Houses*, and make vows. I carry them out with respect and my heart.

Guan Yin Bodhisattva has helped me with my problems: health, work, money, life opportunities, and relatives.

Now I'm very happy because I live a peaceful life and all my problems were solved.

Thank you, Greatly Merciful and Greatly Compassionate Guan Yin Bodhisattva.

You can see from my 53-year-old face that now I look calm, happy and healthy because I follow the teachings of Master Lu, who has helped millions of people to access to the truth of life and receive the blessings of the Great Guan Yin Bodhisattva over 10 years.

Master Lu has done a lot to promote peace, Chinese culture and language, relations with China and of course peaceful and respectful Buddhism.

He is a great Buddhist because he practises charity and has given a lot of money to help people.

All these conferences all over the world, all the food we eat, and those delicious dishes are free!

Do you know anyone who would do things for others for free, and just simply want them to be happy, to have a good life and good health, and to go Heaven? The only person I know who does— that is Master Lu!

Like you, I love him. He is my Master, my Father and my Professor.

By following his teachings, attending his public talks on Buddhism and practicing Guan Yin Citta Dharma door, we will find the great happiness.

I hope everyone here does their best to promote Guan Yin Citta Dharma Door, Buddhism, vegetarianism, peace, Master Lu's Oriental Radio and their websites.

Thank you, Guan Yin Bodhisattva.
Thank you, Master Lu

The world needs you.

I hope all of you do your best to introduce this great Dharma Door and Guan Yin Bodhisattva to a lot of people who are interested in the wisdom of Buddhism and traditional Chinese culture.

My deep gratitude to Great Bodhisattva
My deep gratitude to Guan Yin Bodhisattva
My deep gratitude to Bodhisattvas
My deep gratitude to Master Lu
Thank you to all of you.

Shi Xin Wu
2017

2. Guan Yin Citta Dharma Door Saves My Life from Predestined Calamities

I express my deepest gratitude to the Greatly Merciful and Greatly Compassionate Guan Yin Bodhisattva!

My deepest gratitude to all Buddhas and Bodhisattvas and Dharma Protectors!

My deepest gratitude to Master Jun Hong Lu!

My deepest gratitude to all!

Today, I would like to share how Guan Yin Bodhisattva and Guan Yin Citta Dharma Door helped me to overcome the obstacles I was predestined to encounter. I started following Master Lu in learning Buddhism and cultivating myself in 2015 and it has been 3 years since then. My journey in learning Buddhism has been smooth sailing as Guan Yin Bodhisattva, who grants all wishes, has blessed me with good fortune in all my endeavours. At the end of 2017, I met with my predestined karmic obstacles. Hence, I met with a series of accidents.

On 5 December 2017, I got into an accident with a vehicle belonging to the Singapore Ministry of Foreign Affairs while driving. Back then, it was only the bonnet of the car that was damaged while both parties were unhurt. I knew that it was Guan Yin Bodhisattva that protected me. Deepest gratitude to Guan Yin Bodhisattva! Nevertheless, the karmic obstacles were not yet over.

Less than two weeks after this accident, on 17 December 2017, which was the second night after I got my car from the garage, I heard a loud scream from a pedestrian when I was about to take a turn at an intersection. The next thing I knew, glass shards from the car fell all over my body and a motorcycle crashed into my car door on the left. It was at that moment where I saw a lady on the left of my car knocked into the air and landed on the right, and I was stunned by this scene. In my heart, I kept praying to Guan Yin Bodhisattva while getting off the car to check. I saw a man whose face was covered with blood, with gouging eyes, lying motionless on the ground. The injured lady crawled over from the other side to check the man's injuries. I was trembling all over and couldn't even turn on my phone.

When the police and ambulance arrived, my mind went blank. After having my statement recorded, I returned home to wait for further notice. I didn't know how the police would determine the outcome of this accident, as the law in Singapore tends to favour pedestrians over drivers. If the outcome showed that I was at fault, I would be fined a large amount or face criminal prosecution.

When I reached home, I knelt in front of Guan Yin Bodhisattva and crying bitterly, begged for forgiveness. I made vows to recite *Little Houses*, perform recitation to resolve negative karmic affinities and life liberation. I also used merits from attending Master Lu's public talks to resolve this calamity. This was done in hope of getting Bodhisattva's forgiveness. However, there was not a night I could sleep well after that accident, when I closed my eyes, I could see that victim covered in blood. I could not eat or sleep and had to bear the daily torture of fear and anxiety. Whenever the phone rang, I would be afraid that it was from the police or the hospital delivering bad news. My emotional state was at an all-time low.

While awaiting the outcome of the police investigation, the level of stress and helplessness was indescribable. I didn't wish to talk about this incident with the people around me, but relied on listening to Master Lu's *Buddhism in Plain Terms* to pass my days. If not because of the spiritual energy and blessings from reading *Buddhism in Plain Terms*, I would have collapsed in no time. One day, I saw a line from *Buddhism in Plain Terms* which says that, "Buddhas will respond to those who are sincere. If a person is sincere in changing for the better, Buddhas and Bodhisattvas will definitely respond'. When I saw this line, the Dharma body of Master Lu immediately appeared in my mind, severely reprimanding me by saying, "Regardless of whether this cause was created in your past or present life, now that you have experienced such karmic retribution, why haven't you sincerely repented to Guan Yin Bodhisattva!" My tears started flowing uncontrollably and the pain was so intense that I wished I was dead. I immediately knelt in front of Guan Yin Bodhisattva to repent and made a vow to recite the **Eighty-Eight Buddhas Great Repentance** to repent for the causes that I had created in my past life that resulted in such karmic retribution. It was only then did I realise the reason behind why I had been unable to calm my mind despite having performed so much recitation and offering so many *Little Houses*. I only knew how to make vows, perform recitation and life liberation. However, I did not sincerely repent to Bodhisattva and admit my mistakes through reciting the *Eighty-Eight Buddhas Great Repentance* for the wrongs I did. Deepest gratitude to Master Lu's Dharma body for saving me once again.

In January this year, I received a reply from the police mentioning that due to the lack of surveillance at the place of the accident and inadequate eyewitness accounts, they were unable to determine who was the responsible party. I would not be prosecuted for the time being, but the case would be handed over to court. The police wanted me to be mentally prepared for the worst-case scenario as Singaporean judges tend to favour riders and pedestrians who sustain serious injuries in accidents. My chances of winning were only at 20% to 30%. I was in the depths of despair once again and cried bitterly about the karmic causes I had created in my past life, such that I had to bear the karmic retribution of this traffic accident in this life.

In February, I attended Master Lu's public talk on Buddhism in Sydney. It was as if Master Lu knew about the pain in my heart, he came forward to bless me by placing his palm on my forehead. Master Lu's compassion made me feel deep remorse. I then made a vow to cultivate diligently so to not let Master Lu down.

I performed recitation and repented of my wrongdoing. Finally, I receive notice from police this April. It said that because the police had no evidence to show that I was responsible for the car accident, the police and the court would not charge me.

Both sides just need to pay for their own insurance and maintenance.

My deepest gratitude to Bodhisattva for showing compassion towards me, my deepest gratitude to Master Lu for never leaving me and ensuring that I am safe and sound!

During the 6 months awaiting trial, I decided to try and obtain a taxi license to support my family. However, to obtain a taxi license in Singapore, the Land Transport Authority needs to check your driving record. If record shows that you have flouted serious traffic rules, your application for the license may be rejected. I was extremely worried that the traffic incident would affect the license application, as it was such a serious case. However, I still have a child to care for, thus obtaining the license was extremely important to me.

I then thought about praying to Guan Yin Bodhisattva for blessing in obtaining the taxi license and vowed to release 500 fish which were on the verge of being killed. Each time I would personally drive from Singapore to the market in Malaysia to buy fish that would otherwise have been killed and liberate them at a nearby river. I also vowed to recite several batches of *Little Houses*, with each batch containing 21 pieces, and the **Cundi Dharani** 108 times every day. This was done to seek Guan Yin Bodhisattva's blessing for the application process. At the same time, I also applied for a ridesharing driver's license. Through the Three Golden Buddhist Practices of Guan Yin Citta Dharma Door, I successfully obtained both licenses. If I didn't have the blessings of Guan Yin Bodhisattva, I wouldn't have been able to accomplish this due to the recent accident. My deepest gratitude to the Greatly Merciful and Greatly Compassionate Guan Yin Bodhisattva.

After this car accident, I was anxious to sell my car. Through performing recitation, making vows and performing life liberation, I was able to quickly find a buyer, and selling it at one thousand dollars more than my expectation. This was just enough to cover the compensation to the insurance company. My deepest gratitude to the Greatly Merciful and Greatly Compassionate Guan Yin Bodhisattva.

From this car accident, I realised the importance of reading *Buddhism in Plain Terms* and merits from attending Master Lu's public talks allow me to disperse calamities. I am able to stand before you today due to chances granted by Bodhisattva. The above constitutes my sharing. I express my deepest gratitude to the Greatly Merciful and Greatly Compassionate Guan Yin Bodhisattva for protecting me from such major incidents. My deepest gratitude to Master Lu! My deepest gratitude to all!

Anqi Zhu
2018

3. Three years ago, my doctor said to me, "people with this disease do not survive beyond two years".

I express my deepest gratitude to the Greatly Merciful and Greatly Compassionate Guan Yin Bodhisattva!
My deepest gratitude to all Buddhas and Bodhisattvas!
My deepest gratitude to Master Jun Hong Lu!

First and foremost, I would like to express my gratitude for being given the opportunity to share with you my story today. I thank Guan Yin Citta Dharma Door and the Greatly Merciful and Greatly Compassionate Guan Yin Bodhisattva for helping me to pull through the calamity that had befallen me.

On 12th January 2012, I went for a check-up at XinHua Hospital Shanghai, due to severe influenza and cough. The result, coupled with a CT scan, indicated signs of hardening in the lower half of my lung. I proceeded with a biopsy scan, again it was confirmed to be moderate interstitial pneumonia. According to the doctor, this is one of the rarest and chronic pneumonia. The chances of contracting it is one in ten thousand pneumonia patients. There is no cure to it and patients have to depend on steroids. I was hospitalized for 42 days. Once I returned home, I was prescribed with various types of steroids, which caused serious damage to my immune system.

After one and a half years, I discovered that both my legs had lost the strength to walk. In June 2014, I sought consultation from an orthopaedic surgeon. I was told that my condition was due to the bone death of femoral head. In order to regain the strength to walk, it's highly recommended that I go for a transplant of an imported artificial femoral head. Which would cost me 200,000 RMB, but it could only last for 15 years. In other words, when I am 65 years old, I have to undergo another transplant. I was trembling in fear. Not wanting to be confined to a wheelchair for the rest of my life, I accepted the recommendation. During the process of registration, the doctors found that my lungs were not well, so I was sent for a test to determine if I was fit for the operation.

The pulmonary competency test was conducted on 24th June. My interstitial pneumonia condition had worsened. I was admitted to hospital again. Due to the intake of heavy dosage of steroids over a long period of time, I suffered bone death both sides of the femoral head. I was diagnosed with hypoxemia, i.e. an abnormally low concentration of oxygen in the blood. Wearing a medical oxygen respirator was my only option to increase the oxygen level in the blood, or I would just pass out. Due to a low oxygen concentration in the blood, my palms and fingers turned blue, the skin around my body, ears and knees were shedding off. Even my fingertips were always on medical adhesive plaster to prevent the skin from shedding off. Every morning the hospital staff had to replace my bed sheet as there were small flakes of dead skin on it. My family members were at their wits' end, so they went to the temple and did all sorts of Buddhist rituals for me.

I was discharged from hospital two weeks later. The doctor

said I had only 2 years to live. He told me to go home to eat whatever I like. The chance to survive beyond 3 years is only 20%. Every three months, I had to return to hospital for treatment. At home, I equipped myself with respiratory equipment as I had to have it on all the time. I would have to gasp for breath if I removed the device for a short while to have a shower or even brush my teeth. I was left all alone at home crying when my family left for work. I lamented why a kind person would have to suffer like this in the middle of the night. I had nightmares almost every night. Constantly, I could hear voices calling out my name.

A Buddhist friend from Tianjin happened to be aware of my dilemma and approached me. She asked if I believe in Buddhism. She introduced Guan Yin Citta Dharma Door to me, emphasizing that many cancer patients had recovered through performing recitation. Two days later, she posted some books to me. I was still in doubt at that moment. As a result of severe hypoxemia, my entire body was weak, and I had to put the book aside. A week later, I approached a good friend for help, she read the books and came over to teach me. This is how both of us embarked on the journey of practicing Buddhism.

In the beginning, I had to lie down to perform scripture recitation while breathing through the medical oxygen respirator. After few days, I could literally sit up and recite for a couple of minutes. A week later, I was able to sit up and recite for a good one hour. I could also complete one *Little House* in less than two days. One and a half months later, I did not need to lie down anymore. Right now, I wake up at 6 in the morning, sit by the balcony around 8am and perform recitation while basking in the sunlight, I can easily complete one *Little House* a day.

As a beginner without proper guidance, I had zero knowledge about the steps and routines to daily recitations. To complete *Little House* on a daily basis was my only goal. After completing the *Little Houses*, I had no idea how to keep a record, I did not offer them in a proper way. In March 2015, I was introduced to Ms Tang who taught me the right way of reciting Buddhist scriptures, making vows, and performing life liberation. On the day we met, I vowed to complete 1000 *Little Houses* by 31st December 2016, to be on a vegetarian diet for 15 days a month, and to liberate 10,000 fish (so far I have liberated 5000 fish). I have also reorganised my daily recitation routine: The **Heart Sutra** 49 times, the **Great Compassion Mantra** 49 times, the *Eighty-Eight Buddhas Great Repentance* 5 times, and also other sutras. On the same night, I dreamt that Master Lu was in a white shirt sitting by my bed.

With the guidance of Ms Tang, I began my daily recitation according to the right method. When I was about to complete 50 *Little Houses*, I regained the strength to do simple chores without the respirator. During that period of time, I woke up at 5 a.m. to perform recitation. I could complete two or three *Little Houses* daily. Seeing the great change in me, my family members stopped obstructing me from performing the recitation.

I am well aware that I had a lot of karmic debts. In addition to the daily recitations and *Little Houses*, I repented before Guan Yin Bodhisattva and vowed to recite the **Amitabha Pure Land Rebirth Mantra** 6,000 times and the **Heart Sutra** 2,000 times. My skin condition has improved. Hence, I vowed to offer another similar batch after two and a half months. At present, my skin has stopped shedding off. I no longer need to be on steroids.

In June last year, I was fortunate enough to participate in Master Lu's public talk on Buddhism in Hong Kong. Throughout the talk, even though I was not wearing a respirator, I did not develop any discomfort at all. I could even complete 3 *Little Houses* every day. After returning from Hong Kong, my family and my friends could tell the transformation in me, I look normal now except a little problem with my legs. I stand here today, strong and healthy, to share with you my personal experiences. Guan Yin Citta Dharma Door which has saved my life.

Last but not least, I would like to express my gratitude to the Greatly Merciful and Greatly Compassionate Guan Yin Bodhisattva! Thank you to Master Jun Hong Lu! And dear Buddhist friends, thank you for your attention.

Junqing Gan
2017

4. Guan Yin Citta Dharma Door fulfils my dream of becoming a mother

I express my deep gratitude to the Greatly Merciful and Greatly Compassionate Guan Yin Bodhisattva!
My gratitude to all Buddhas and Bodhisattvas of the ten directors and the three periods of time!
My gratitude to all Dharma Protectors!
My gratitude to Master Jun Hong Lu who has been devoting his life to saving others!

I'm one of Master Lu's disciples, and I come from Shanghai. Due to the infertility after being married for about 10 years, I sought help from both traditional Chinese and Western medicine, underwent countless surgeries, and experienced everything that someone desperately try to have a baby could endure.

In March 2014, I got to know about Guan Yin Citta. In September 2014, I attended Master Lu's public talk on Buddhism in Taiwan along with my mother. The testimony from many fellow practitioners and Master Lu's compassionate teachings lightened me up. I began to understand my suffering was caused by my heavy karmic debts accumulated in my past and present lives. I knelt in front of Guan Yin Bodhisattva and vowed with tears in my eyes that, "I will recite 108 *Little Houses* for my karmic creditors, and release 5000 fish by the end of December. I'll follow Master Lu in practising Guan Yin Citta Dharma door diligently to recite sutras, release fish and help more people spiritually awaken by learning Buddhism. " In that way, I believe that I will have my wish to have my own children fulfilled. In October 2014, not long after I went back to Shanghai from the public talk in Taiwan, I suddenly came down with the chicken pox, which is infectious. I could not go outside or go to work. I had to rest at home. It suddenly occurred to me that my work at the bank was busy all day. So how would it be possible for me to complete the 108 *Little Houses* within the time frame that I promised? I just learned to recite sutras not long ago. I realised that it was a blessing and compassion from the Guanyin Bodhisattva and Master Lu who gave me such an opportunity to recite *Little Houses* quietly at home.

In May 2015, I came across a specialist from the Shanghai International Peace Maternal and Child Health Hospital. I had never met someone who as amiable as her during the past nine years of seeking treatment. Apart from that, we have the same religious beliefs and common interests. The doctor asked me to adhere to a vegetarian diet, just like the children who grow up in the rural areas who could not afford expensive meals and so they were only limited to simple meals every day. It was the compassionate blessing from Guan Yin Bodhisattva and Master Lu that I could encounter such a good doctor. I firmly believe that Guan Yin Bodhisattva makes the best arrangement for us if we have total faith in her.

In December 2015, my mother attended Master Lu's public talk on Buddhism in Penang, Malaysia, where Master Lu said

"Anyone who has participated in this event can transfer part of the merits to the family members so that their diseases can be cured and wishes fulfilled". At the night, my mother knelt in front of Guan Yin Bodhisattva and prayed: "I'm willing to transfer 50% of the merits gained from assisting Master Lu's public talk to my daughter. May the Greatly Merciful and Greatly Compassionate Guan Yin Bodhisattva bless my daughter to get pregnant to fulfil her wish of becoming a mother. We promise we will share this experience with people and help them spiritually awaken by learning Buddhism."

In January 2016, I was found to be pregnant. On October 20th, 2016, I gave birth to a 3.3-kg baby girl through a smooth caesarean section. We have raised the baby girl as a vegetarian since birth.

How time flies! My lovely vegetarian baby girl is already nine months old. It is proved that a vegetarian baby will not lack nutrition and will grow healthily and happily as long as the mother insists on breastfeeding and eats balanced vegetarian meals.

It is not easy to be born human. Even when we have attained this, it still remains unusual that we will get the chance to learn Buddhist teachings, but now we have this rare opportunity. For those who have not had faith in Guan Yin Citta Dharma Door and those who have not yet started to recite sutras, I'd like to say that it is a truly great blessing that we could be able to hear the Dharma and meet our Master. Guan Yin Citta Dharma Door is bestowed by Guan Yin Bodhisattva. By applying the Three Golden Buddhist Practices which include performing life liberation, making great vows and reciting sutras and mantras in our daily lives, our diseases will be cured and problems will be solved. Guan Yin Citta Dharma Door is truly effective. By assisting in the public talk, we can help ourselves to remove negative karma, help others spiritually awaken and accumulate merits and virtues. When necessary, we can use the merits to help our family members. This is priceless and invaluable. I sincerely hope that we do not miss such a good method of Buddhist practice, and cherish the blessings and positive affinity we have with Buddhism.

That was all for my story. If there are any inappropriate remarks in my testimony, I ask for forgiveness from the Greatly Merciful and Greatly Compassionate Guan Yin Bodhisattva, from the Dharma Protectors, from Master Lu and from all of you.

My deepest gratitude to the Greatly Merciful and Greatly Compassionate Guan Yin Bodhisattva!
My deepest gratitude to all the Dharma Protectors who guard this Buddhist event.
My deepest gratitude to Master Jun Hong Lu!
My gratitude to my mother who has been supporting me all my life.
My gratitude to fellow practitioners from Guan Yin Citta who have been helping me and teaching me. Gratitude to the fellow practitioners who recited the *Great Compassion Mantra* for me when I was underging the caesarean section!

Ting Yu
2017

5. My extraordinary experience of practising Guan Yin Citta Dharma Door in France

Hello everyone. With tremendous joy and sincerest homage to Master Lu, I travelled all the way from France to attend this solemn event.

My name is Jean Louis Felicité and I live in Cannes, a city in the south of France. My ancestors were from Mauritius. I have always had a strong interest in Buddhism and Asian culture, and I often visit temples and live in the temples for a period of time. Many people say that when I recite Buddhist scriptures, my pronunciation is as good as a native Chinese speaker. Therefore, I believe that I have a deep affinity with Buddhism.

I have practised Guan Yin Citta Dharma Door for two years. My friend Mr Wong runs a shop in Cannes where I got my first book and started to recite Buddhist scriptures. At the beginning, troubled by too many trivial matters in life, I wasn't persistent in my practice. Not long after that, I encountered massive problems including divorce, unemployment, illness and financial stress.

After reading other practitioners' sharing and watching Master Lu's Totem-reading videos, I was stunned by Master Lu's spiritual power, and the inspirational effects of Guan Yin Citta — It is a Dharma Door which is very easy to practice. I attempted to attend Master Lu's public talk twice in 2017. One was in Italy, and the other one was in Paris. However, due to some obstacles at the last minute, I failed to make the trip happen on both occasions, which saddened me to tears.

With the advice of other practitioners, I came to the realisation that the condition for me to attend these public talks had not ripened; I hadn't recited enough *Little Houses* to pay off my negative karma.

At the beginning of this year, I finally understood that all misfortunes I experienced were the retributions of the negative karma I created in the past. What matters the most now is to perform life liberation and recitation of *Little Houses* to eliminate my karmic debts. I was determined to practise Guan Yin Citta Dharma Door with great diligence. On the 1st and 15th of each lunar month, I liberated live seafood with other Buddhist friends. I have also become persistent in reciting *Little Houses* for my karmic creditors. I can now recite one *Little House* per day and have completed more than 30 *Little Houses* so far.

The first life liberation was a very memorable experience for me. After performing rituals and releasing seafood into the sea, my body started to tremble, and I felt a stream of warm and cold currents travelling through my body. My Buddhist friends noticed that I had had some marvellous feelings. The day after that, I felt very weak and tired as though my entire body had been cleaned thoroughly. My Buddhist friends said that I received great blessings from Guan Yin Bodhisattva.

In January 2018, with the help of other practitioners, I attended the blessing ceremony of the local Guan Yin Citta

Buddhist Practice Centre in Austria. The trip was a solemn pilgrimage to me. I interacted a lot with Master Lu's disciples. Again, I felt a substantial energy in the ceremony and even after I returned home, my heart was still filled with such positive energy.

Following such blessings, I had major surgery on my knee the next day. It was a very complicated surgery and caused a lot of pain. I stayed in the hospital for four months. With the encouragement of my Buddhist friends, I never gave up and continued to be diligent in reciting scriptures and making prayers. My recovery was so quick and so well that it stunned my doctor. I knew that it was all attributed to the firm belief I held in Guan Yin Bodhisattva. Take a look, I have now fully recovered!

I am very grateful to Guan Yin Bodhisattva, who gave me her blessings to overcome obstacles happening in my life. Finally, I am able to attend Master Lu's public talk this time after a 15-hour flight from France, fulfilling the wish that I have been longing for. I am very delighted to be here with all of you today. I have a strong faith in Guan Yin Bodhisattva and I will persevere in my practice with great determination and belief. My sincere gratitude to Guan Yin Bodhisattva for accepting me and never giving up on me. The more devout and sincere I am, the more courageous and energetic I feel, which helps me to achieve inner peace and purification of mind.

I express my deepest gratitude towards the Greatly Merciful and Greatly Compassionate Guan Yin Bodhisattva!

My deepest gratitude towards Master Lu!

My deepest gratitude towards all Buddhist practitioners who guided me into the noble path of Buddhist practice.

Jean Louis Félicite
2017

The original script in French below:

Bonjour à tous, c'est avec une immense joie que je porte dans le cœur pour venir assister à la conférence du Maître Lu, auquel je porte toutes mes admirations et respect.

Je m'appelle Jean Louis Felicité, j'habite à Cannes, et je suis d'origine mauricienne, je suis toujours très attiré par tout ce qui est bouddhisme et culture asiatique, j'aime fréquenter les temples bouddhistes et y faire un séjour et quand je récite les soutras, tout le monde me dit que je prononce le texte aussi bien qu'un chinois. Donc j'ai beaucoup d'affinité avec le bouddhisme.

Cela fait deux ans que je pratique la Porte de Dharma Guan Yin Citta. Mon ami Wong qui tient une boutique de Feng Shui à Canne m'a initié à cette pratique, j'ai commencé à réciter les soutras, comme à l'époque j'étais assez occupé, je n'ai pas pratiqué de façon régulière, et il s'en suit une série de calamité pour ma vie personnelle durant ces deux dernières années : divorce, le chômage, santé et soucis financiers etc.

A travers les témoignages, les vidéos, j'ai vraiment pris conscience de l'incroyable puissance du Maître Lu et et l'efficacité de cette pratique simple. J'ai essayé à deux prises de venir assister aux conférences de Maître Lu l'année dernière 2017, la première en Italie et la deuxième à Paris, comme s'il y avait un barrage, un empêchement au dernier moment pour que je ne puisse être présent pour cet évènement, j'ai pleuré de désespérance.

Grâce aux explications des pratiquants, j'ai compris que je n'étais pas encore prêt parce que je n'avais pas assez récité de Petite-Maison pour nettoyage de tous les mauvais karmas du passé.

Et depuis début de cette année, j'ai compris que tous les problèmes que j'ai rencontré dans ma vie sont liés au karma négatif du passé, et l'essentiel est de réduire ce stock de karma en libérant les vies et en récitant les Petites-Maisons. Donc j'ai commencé sérieusement cette fois-ci la pratique : on lâche des moules tous les 1 et 15 ème du mois avec d'autres pratiquants, et je récite régulièrement les Petites-Maisons, au total j'ai récité une trentaine de Petites-Maisons, je peux maintenant faire une par jour .

La première fois que je pratiquais le rituel de libération de vie, c'était une expérience inoubliable, nous avons lâché des moules au bord de la mer. Juste après le rituel de récitation, et lâché des moules, j'ai commencé à avoir une étrange sensation de sueur chaude et froide à l'intérieur de tout mon corps avec des tremblements que j'ai pu montrer à mes amis à côtés. Et après pendant toute la journée je me sentais très très faible , épuisé , nettoyé et vidé de tout. Tout le monde me disait que j'étais fortement béni par Guan Yin.

Au Janvier 2018, grâce aux aides des pratiquants, j'ai pu participer à l'inauguration de la Maison de Guan Yin d'Autriche, ce voyage à Vienne était un grand pèlerinage pour moi, j'ai beaucoup échangé avec les disciples du Maître Lu, et je ressentais une énergie tellement forte dans la Maison de Guan Yin à Vienne, et quand je suis rentré, je me sens rempli de lumière au cœur.

Grâce à cette bénédiction, j'ai pu faire face à une opération chirurgicale du genou très lourde et très douloureuse. J'étais hospitalisé pendant quatre mois et grâce à l'encouragements de mes amis bouddhistes, je n'ai pas baissé le bras, tous les jours, je récite, et faire la prière, et le médecin était très étonné de cette vitesse de guérison en moi qui est beaucoup plus rapide que la norme générale. Je sais que tout cela est lié à ma croyance de Guan Yin. Regardez, je suis maintenant entièrement rétabli !! Merci au Boddhisattva Guan Yin qui m'a donné cette force pour vaincre les difficultés de ma vie.

Enfin, j'ai pu effectuer cette fois-ci ce pèlerinage tant désiré et tant attendu pour venir voir Maître Lu, Je suis très heureux aujourd'hui d'être parmi vous , après un si long voyage de 15hrs de vol de France. J'ai la conviction que je vais encore aller plus loin dans ma croyance de Guan Yin. Mille gratitudes au Boddhisattva Guan Yin de m'avoir accepté. Plus je pratique la Petite-Maison, avec beaucoup de croyance et de foi, plus cela me donne de la force spirituelle et encore plus de courage de retrouver la paix intérieurement de moi dans le calme.

Mille Gratitude au Boddhisattva Guan Yin, Mille gratitude au Maître Lu, Mille gratitude à ceux qui m'ont guidé dans cette voie.

Jean Louis Félicite
2017

6. Guan Yin Citta Dharma Door Saves My Life and Marriage

I express my deep gratitude to the Greatly Merciful and Greatly Compassionate Guan Yin Bodhisattva.

My gratitude to the Buddhas, Bodhisattvas and Dharma Protectors.

My gratitude to Master Jun Hong Lu.

My name is Wang Hui Ping from Shandong, China. I'm 50 years old. I started to practise Guan Yin Citta Dharma Door in March 2015. Guan Yin Citta Dharma Door has changed my life and my family! I would like to share with you my experience of practicing Guan Yin Citta for more than two years, and the benefits I have obtained. If there's anything inappropriate in my story, may Guan Yin Bodhisattva and the Dharma Protectors forgive me. I will bear my own karmic debts and will not let Master Lu bear them for me.

I'm a cancer patient. Before practicing Buddhism, I knew nothing about the law of cause and effect in life. Due to my ignorance, I committed a lot of negative karma. I aborted a 3-month-old foetus in 1993. The karma of the abortion did not ripen until 16 years later when I was diagnosed with cervical cancer in 2009. At that moment, I couldn't believe it. My daughter just entered her first year of high school, how could she live without a mother? Not long after my operation, I had a relationship crisis with my husband. In 2013, we mutually agreed to divorce. During that period, I suffered severe pain in my stomach and lower back during menstruation. I was not aware that this was due to the activation of my negative karma, I thought it was a side effect of the surgery. I consulted specialists many times and begged them to remove my ovaries, womb, and cervix but they refused to do so. I had to continue to bear this excruciating pain, and I was very sick during those days.

The collapse of my marriage and the cancer were like a double blow to me, causing my health to deteriorate. During chemotherapy, I had to bear with bladder and bowel dysfunction. The doctor treated me with a big electric acupuncture needle throughout the chemotherapy process regularly. My body became so fragile that I couldn't stand and walk steadily. On my return from work, I needed someone in front of me to pull me and someone at the back to push me up in order for me to get onto the bus. My condition worsened to the extent that I was too weak to work. All these pains caused me to keep thinking of ending my life. There was always a voice whispering to me, "Jump down from a higher floor. You live on the 9th floor which is too low, follow me right now....". Mentally, I had completely collapsed. I went to a few established hospitals for a check-up, and the Doctors told me that I was suffering from severe depression. I couldn't fall asleep for countless nights. I sat beside my child, looking at her, sleeping like a baby, and I wept uncontrollably. Then, I thought about my 80-year-old parents, whom I owe a deep debt of gratitude and should fulfil my filial responsibility. I can't bring myself to let them see me leave this world before them.

With the compassion of the Bodhisattva, at the end of 2014, Ms Lee from Xian introduced me to a group of practitioners of Guan Yin Citta Dharma Door. Master Lu's public talk on Buddhism and Totem reading had a great impact on me. I started to understand the truth behind many things, which enabled me to realize the existence of the law of cause and effect. I came to realize that I have committed a lot of mistakes, and I began to repent. With the blessing of Guan Yin Bodhisattva, I gave up the attempt of suicide. I decided to diligently perform recitation, cultivate good behaviour, repent and reduce my karmic debts.

Guan Yin Citta Dharma Door is truly effective. I persistently performed recitation, life liberation and made vows for about 3 months, and then my health improved significantly. The symptoms of my depression lessened. The blessing of the Bodhisattva had given me more confidence in practising Buddhism.

With the help of Ms Ji from Germany, Ms Chen from Beijing and Ms Yan, I vowed to adopt a full vegetarian diet for the rest of my life. In July 2016, I attended the Public Talk in Hong Kong, during which I saw Guan Yin Bodhisattva and Master Lu. My tears couldn't stop flowing. I knelt down in front of Bodhisattva and repented my wrongdoing, I begged for forgiveness from Guan Yin Bodhisattva!

Before November 2016, after reciting about 700 *Little Houses*, I recovered from depression, chronic waist pain, headache, years of bladder and bowel dysfunction, severe insomnia and other illnesses.

In December 2016, I went for a medical check-up, the specialist that performed the surgery on me was amazed by the results of my medical report. He was excited and told me that those results were all 'normal'. I was so grateful to Guan Yin Bodhisattva and Master Jun Hong Lu!

Before practicing Buddhism, I used to be hot-tempered and found others unpleasant. After practising Buddhism, my family members and friends said that I had changed a lot. On top of that, I was surprised and overjoyed when my ex-husband asked to get back together with me. I urged him to stop smoking and drinking. I advised him to practise Buddhism together with me. He started to perform recitation, we remarried each other in January 2017. The blessing of Guan Yin Bodhisattva and Master Jun Hong Lu brought back my happy family!

I made vows in front of Guan Yin Bodhisattva on 10th November 2016 that I would recite 1000 *Little Houses* for my karmic creditors and release 10,000 fish within a year. Day and night without fail, I performed recitation before my Buddhist altar. When I was sleepy I would doze off for a while and then continue to perform the recitation. I wanted to finish reciting the 1000 *Little Houses* two and a half months before Master Lu's public talk in Malaysia. On 17th August, I completed the 1000 *Little Houses*. I have recited about 1700 *Little Houses* within two and a half years. My life is not easy, but I managed to release 10,000 fish by April 2017. On 8th June 2017, I made a vow again, I would share my experience of practicing Guan Yin Citta Dharma Door 100 times through the Internet and social media. I wanted to spread the messages of Buddhism and reach out to more sentient beings. To date, I have shared my Buddhism experience 173 times, exceeding the number that I had promised.

Thanks to Guan Yin Bodhisattva and Master Jun Hong Lu, I have let go of resentments, doubts and greed. I give thanks to Guan Yin Citta Dharma Door for giving me a new lease on life, good health and hope. It has changed my life from despair to hope, from darkness to brightness! From now on, I must continue to perform the Three Golden Buddhist Practices of Guan Yin Citta Dharma Door: making vows, reciting scriptures and performing life liberation. I will learn from the respectable Master Lu, help people to practise Buddhism, be a diligent Buddhist practitioner and make full use of this life to transcend the cycle of rebirth!

My deepest gratitude to the Greatly Merciful and Greatly Compassionate Guan Yin Bodhisattva!
My deepest gratitude to all Buddhas and Dharma Protectors!
My deepest gratitude to Master Jun Hong Lu!
My deepest gratitude to all volunteers and Buddhist friends for allowing me to share my story today. Should there be anything inappropriate in my story, I beg for forgiveness from Bodhisattvas, Dharma Protectors, Master and everyone. Thank You!

Huiping Wang
2017

7. I just got my GCE 'O'Level result as I hoped!

I got the exact result I prayed for in my GCE O Level Exam!

Growing up, I was rather indifferent towards religion. The idea of a God was one I would avoid discussing partly due to the fact I didn't believe in Him and also partly because I didn't want to offend God if He really existed.

My mum got to know about Guan Yin Citta when I was in Secondary Four. She almost immediately started reciting Buddhist scriptures when she entered the Dharma Door. I was reserved and didn't want to meddle in such religious practices at first. But one faithful day before my common test, I went up to my mum and asked for the mantra book. I just started reciting using "Hanyu pinyin" despite the fact that I couldn't read much Chinese. At that point I was probably tired from all the revision and needed a break, and the recitation did the job. Why not sleep you may ask? Because my mum nagging me to sleep always happens the day before a test. As for the results of my common test, it came out rather well. Since then, I started chanting every day. After a while, I increased the number of daily recitations of the *Great Compassion Mantra* to 7, *Heart Sutra* to 7, and Cundi Dharani to 21. A few months before my O level, I increased my recitation of the Cundi Dharani to 49!

I was at a neighbourhood secondary school which had 2 mock

O level exams before our actual O levels. My exam results for the two mock ones were not ideal at all, even though small improvements were made between the two. In the last mock exam, I got a L1R2B2 of 18 and a L1R5 of 22, which were very worrying for those who know the grading system for O levels. After each time studying the mock exam, I gained more knowledge. In the meantime, I went through the possibilities of what could happen to me. The worst-case scenario was that I would end up in the ITE. Was it something I wanted? No. But it's something I could deal with. That small session made me realise that failure isn't the end, the people I love would still be around, and there is really nothing much I have to fear about getting bad results. Once I dismissed my fear and stress, I went full steam ahead and studied hard, finding myself able to leave my phone and other distractions aside and actually study for the first time. This wisdom and motivation I guess was from Guan Yin Bodhisattva.

I prayed every day for a L1R2B2 of 8 points and I got the exact same marks for all 4 types of L1R2B2 and with a L1R2B2 of 8. My L1R5 was naturally good, and I got 11 points for that.

Could I have gotten a better result? I don't think so. At 16 years of age in the 21st century, I think I did exceptionally well, considering my starting point in Sec 1, having appealed to my secondary school, and being the last in the whole of the school (my results now belong in the top 30% of my school). Sleep, ample rest and knowing when to stop and relax were what I think I did correct this time, and my daily recitation was what kept me going. The praying and recitation every day filled my down time and kept me away from play and social media. Apparently, my prayers were heard, and Guan Yin Bodhisattva granted me the results I prayed for!

If a religion could reward me with exactly what I wanted in less than a year, imagine how a lifetime of following can benefit me. But then again, the teachings of Bodhisattva say that you need to realise that ultimately all the material gains you obtained will not last forever, they're nothing when life reached its end, and only those who have made a great impact can become immortalized in their works and in the minds of admirers. We should always leave a place better than we found it, aim to right whatever wrongs we can and leave it a better place for others to live in. We should not just complain and whine about all the things we don't like in life and then leave, wondering why things are always so unjust.

You can be like me, start praying to Guan Yin Bodhisattva and start reciting scriptures. Like any other religion, all you need to do is to truly believe and put your faith in it. Sincerely hold onto the belief in Bodhisattva, and then your prayers will be answered. Even if you are not yet ready to join a religion like me, I hope you can do something that has value in your life, help people in need, and treat your friends and family with love and kindness.

J Low
2016

8. Perseverance with Guan Yin Citta Dharma Door Saved My Mother and Changes My Life

I express my deepest gratitude to the Greatly Merciful and Greatly Compassionate Guan Yin Bodhisattva.

My deepest gratitude to Buddhas and Bodhisattvas and Dharma Protectors, Deepest gratitude to Master Jun Hong Lu.

My deepest gratitude to all volunteers and our fellow practitioners.

Good evening! My name is Liu Ben Fang. In 2006, when I was 19 years old, I was diagnosed with dengue fever. Just as Master Lu always reminds us, "We are likely to experience predestined hardships or even calamites when the last digit of our age ends with a 3, 6 or 9."

During that time, I was in great pain, and experienced untold torment physically and mentally. I had fever and felt cold, suffering vomiting, diarrhoea and even incontinence. Despite my serious condition, my father refused to let me seek medical treatment. Later, with the help of an aunt, I was hospitalised for three days and I got well after that. But dengue fever is an illness which is difficult to recover from fully. It can relapse at any time. My lungs, liver, digestive system, and heart have been damaged.

So even though the illness hasn't relapsed, I often have dizziness, headache, pain in the stomach and limbs. This made me resent my family. Why did they treat me this way? Since then, I've suffered a relapse once every two years. I am in great pain. Moreover, numerous incidents have occurred, such as car accidents. My arms were injured in a car accident, and it led to the sequela. The illness and family unhappiness made me feel like I was living in hell, I even thought of committing suicide.

In March 2015, I came across a video of Master Lu's Dharma talk on Facebook. I was sceptical at the time and deliberated whether to give it a try and learn more about this Buddhist practice. However, I was not sure if I had the time to learn because my work was so busy. Also, I had no sense of Buddhist practice and still harboured doubts about it.

In spite of my wavering faith, one month later, I finally visited the Guan Yin Citta Buddhist Practice Centre in Singapore. After the visit, I began to learn daily recitation of Buddhist scriptures and started the practise. Gradually, I came to realise that all the misfortune in this life is attributed to the law of cause and effect. One's suffering is all caused by one's actions – you reap what you sow!

After reciting Buddhist scriptures, my condition improved significantly in 2014. It was actually the period where my illness would recur, but this time I was not struck by the usual pain I used to suffer. I regained my confidence to live on. When hearing this, you might think that it must be credited to my diligent Buddhist practise. But the truth was, due to lack of wisdom, I was still wavering in my faith. Everyone around me – including my colleagues, friends and family- were all unsupportive of my Buddhist practice. They made many unpleasant remarks. In addition, I worked long hours, so it was difficult for me to make time to perform recitation. I began to fall behind in my daily recitations and stopped reciting *Little Houses*. Soon after that, the symptoms of my illness began to show again, and my relationship with colleagues turned bad. I became depressed again and then realized they were all due to my mistakes.

Yielding to people's criticism would only cause me pain. I cried in front of Guan Yin Bodhisattva and sought forgiveness. After I started performing my recitation again I gradually regained strength and reclaimed my health.

In April 2015, I attended Master Lu's public talk in Singapore. I was very lucky to be selected and Master Lu performed a Totem reading for me. Master Lu said my friend's mother who had passed away would be reborn into the family of a relative or a friend in six months. It was absolutely true, because my mother was pregnant at that time and she gave birth to my little sister six months later.

Guan Yin Citta Dharma Door actually saved my mother and my baby sister. My mother was 49 years old when she was pregnant. The doctor detected abnormal viscosity in her blood, so she had to be given haemolytic injections every month.

June 2015 was my mother's expected due date. Due to her old age, her uterus had shrunk, so natural birth was ruled out. If she opted for surgery, she would be at a high risk of postpartum haemorrhage. As she had been receiving blood dilution injections, her life was at risk. At this critical moment, I told my mother, "Mom, make a vow to Guan Yin Bodhisattva, as only Guan Yin Bodhisattva can save you. I vowed to adopt a full vegetarian diet on the 1st day and 15th day of each lunar month and with this merit and virtue, you can seek blessings for a smooth delivery." I also taught her to recite the **Great Compassion Mantra**, the **Heart Sutra**, the Cundi Dharani and the Xiao Zai Ji Xiang Shen Zhou.

On the day of delivery, I accompanied my mother into the delivery room. My mother made this special request to the doctor, saying that I could perform recitations for her. I recited the **Gong De Bao Shan Shen Zhou** and prayed that the merits and virtues from my sister's past life would enable her to be reborn safely. During the surgery, I kept reciting the **Great Compassion Mantra**. It was then that I saw my mom shivering; she was very frightened. With tears streaming down, I said, "Mom you'll be alright, with Guan Yin Bodhisattva's blessing, everything will be alright".

At that time, I had forgotten all my past grievances and resentment towards my parents; I did not wish to lose any of my family members. I felt sorry I had not been a good son. I vowed to be a good son from then on and fulfil my filial responsibilities to them. I kept performing recitation of sutras and mantras while holding my mother's hand tightly.

A miracle happened, the entire surgery went exceptionally well. My sister was delivered safely and there was no sign of haemorrhage. Even the doctor was amazed, claiming that it was a miracle. He had believed that the surgery would cause excessive bleeding. My sister and I are 30 years apart in age. It is the first such age gap on record at the hospital.

My deepest gratitude to Guan Yin Bodhisattva. I have been exposed to many other Buddhist traditions and practices in the past, I have also taken refuge in them. But I have not met such a great Master who has taught me the "Three Golden Buddhist Practices" which enabled me to eliminate my karmic obstacles and change my destiny. There are so many compassionate Buddhist friends who have extended their helping hands.

Before I end my story, I do hope you will believe that Guan Yin Bodhisattva really exists. Guan Yin Bodhisattva is always by our side to bless us. Let us cherish such a rare opportunity to have come across Guan Yin Citta Dharma Door and such a great Master in this lifetime. Together, let us return to the fold of Guan Yin Bodhisattva, who is like a mother in heaven, as that is our real home. That's all I have to share today. If I have said anything inappropriate in my story, I seek forgiveness from the Greatly Merciful and Greatly Compassionate Guan Yin Bodhisattva, all Buddhas and Dharma Protectors.

My deepest gratitude to the Greatly Merciful and Greatly Compassionate Guan Yin Bodhisattva,
My Deepest gratitude to Buddhas and Bodhisattvas and Dharma Protectors,
My deepest gratitude to Master Jun Hong Lu,
My deepest gratitude to all volunteers and Buddhist friends.

Benfang Liu   2017

Postface

For detailed information regarding Master Jun Hong Lu's Guan Yin Citta Dharma Door, please visit Master Lu's websites:

- http://www.GuanYinCitta.com   (English)
- http://lujunhong2or.com   (Chinese)

You can read the entries on **Buddhism in Plain Terms**, **Buddhism: Your Questions Answered**, **Inspirational Stories**, and **Resource Centre**, etc. Please also listen to the recordings of Master Lu's weekly radio programs (Mandarin Chinese), including "The Art of Applying Comprehensive Metaphysics", "Buddhism: Your Questions Answered", and "Buddhism in Plain Terms", as well as recordings from Master Lu's public talks.

Master Lu's radio programs (in Mandarin Chinese):
Note that the broadcast schedule shown below is in Sydney time.

The Art of Applying Comprehensive Metaphysics (Totem Reading)
Every Tuesday, Thursday, and Saturday
5.30pm – 6pm

Buddhism: Your Questions Answered (No Totem Reading)

Every Friday   1pm – 2.30pm

Every Sunday   1pm – 2.30pm

Buddhism in Plain Terms

Every Tuesday, Thursday, and Saturday

5.10pm-5.30pm

Note: Each year, Sydney has the summer Eastern Daylight Time from October to April, and the winter Eastern Standard Time from April to October. If you are trying to call into Master Lu's radio programs, please take Daylight Savings Time into consideration.

Master Lu's Radio Program Hotline: +61 2 9698 8866

Secretariat of Guan Yin Citta Dharma Door: +61 2 9283 2758

Secretariat

Guan Yin Citta Dharma Door

July 2018

Appendix A: Sample *Little House*

OFFERING

O F F E R E D	CHI FO	WANG		TA	O F F
			HSIN		E
	MIEH TSUI	SHENG		PEI	R
			CHING		T
	CHEN YAN	CHOU		CHOU	O :
B Y :					

87 Times   84 Times   49 Times   27 Times

Little Houses can be downloaded from www.GuanYinCitta.com. For more details please refer to another Master Jun Hong Lu's publication: *A Guide to Reciting the Combination of Buddhist Scriptures: Little Houses.*

Appendix B:

Sample *Application for Change of Name*

Application for Change of Name can be downloaded from www.GuanYinCitta.com.

Appendix C:
Sample *Application for True Name*

Sincerely Invite

**The Greatly Merciful and Greatly Compassionate
Guan Yin Bodhisattva**

To Witness:

Devotee's original True Full Name: _____

Current True Full Name: _____

Date of birth: _____ (yyyy/mm/dd)

Devotee's full name: _____

Location: _____

_____ (yyyy/mm/dd)

Application for True Name can be downloaded from www.GuanYinCitta.com.

Appendix D:

Sample *Application for Convincing Family Members* (Caution: Do not burn this form)

Sincerely Invite

The Greatly Merciful and Greatly Compassionate Guan Yin Bodhisattva to bless

Devotee: _____

(full name, date of birth yyyy/mm/dd)

To gain wisdom, believe in Buddhism and start performing recitations

Requested by Devotee: _____

(Please write the devotee's full name. Please do not burn this application)

SAMPLE

Application for Convincing Family Members can be downloaded from www.GuanYinCitta.com.

Generosity

If you would like to support the printing of books by Master Jun Hong Lu, you are welcome to make a donation through any of the following registered charities:

(1) Australia Oriental Media Buddhist Charity Association (St. George Bank)
Bank Name: ST GEORGE BANK
Account Name:
      AUSTRALIA ORIENTAL MEDIA BUDDHIST CHARITY
      ASSOCIATION
BSB Number: 112 879
Account Number: 432 033 033
Swift Code: SGBLAU2S
Bank Address:
    699 GEORGE ST. HAYMARKET NSW 2000 AUSTRALIA
Recipient's Address:
    54 MEAGHER STREET, CHIPPENDALE, NSW 2008
    AUSTRALIA

(2) Australia Oriental Media Buddhist Charity Association (Accepting donations to support the Guan Yin Village project)
Bank Name: ST GEORGE BANK
Account Name:
AUSTRALIA ORIENTAL MEDIA BUDDHIST CHARITY
ASSOCIATION
BSB Number: 112 879
Account Number: 432 919 934
Swift Code: SGBLAU2S
Bank Address:
699 GEORGE ST. HAYMARKET NSW 2000 AUSTRALIA
Recipient's Address:
54 MEAGHER STREET, CHIPPENDALE, NSW 2008 AUSTRALIA

Note: The above accounts are the only ones recognised by the Australia Oriental Media Buddhist Charity Association for the purpose of supporting the printing of Master Lu's books.